the
Tokens

DR. GREG S. REID AND JEFF LEVITAN

the Tokens

11 Lessons
to Help Build
the Foundation of
Success
and Find Your Path
to Greatness

WILEY

Published by John Wiley & Sons, Inc., Hoboken, New Jersey.
Published simultaneously in Canada.

For general information on our other products and services or for technical support, please contact our Customer Care Department within the United States at (800) 762–2974, outside the United States at (317) 572–3993 or fax (317) 572–4002.

Wiley publishes in a variety of print and electronic formats and by print-on-demand. Some material included with standard print versions of this book may not be included in e-books or in print-on-demand. If this book refers to media such as a CD or DVD that is not included in the version you purchased, you may download this material at http://booksupport.wiley.com. For more information about Wiley products, visit www.wiley.com.

Library of Congress Cataloging-in-Publication Data is available:

ISBN 978-1-119-54756-3 (Hardcover)
ISBN 978-1-119-54758-7 (ePDF)
ISBN 978-1-119-54760-0 (ePub)

COVER DESIGN: PAUL McCARTHY
COVER ART: © MMELLO / ISTOCKPHOTO; © TOMOGRAF / ISTOCKPHOTO; © AVNPHOTOLAB / ISTOCKPHOTO

Printed in the United States of America
V10006198_111618

Contents

the
Tokens

Chapter 1

Secrets in the Walls

The trip to town had taken Eric longer than he'd expected. He had set out that morning to run to the hardware store to get some more supplies for the cabin, but one thing had led to another. After a quick stop at the bank, he pulled into the grocery store to replenish some staples—coffee, eggs, bread, and something to throw on the grill for the next couple days should do it. Then he received a call from his boss and had to make a quick run to their job site to meet the drivers who were delivering the roof shingles they needed first thing Monday morning.

When he turned off the main road, it was already midday, and Eric was thinking about how half of his day had been wasted. Another weekend was flying by and he wasn't making much progress on his grandfather's old cabin, but it was a labor of love—particularly because as a boy, during the summers, he had spent a month there with his grandfather. He had enjoyed every minute spent fishing with his grandpa, and now that his grandfather was gone, he intended to spend even more time there. In fact, he was renovating it and building an addition onto the back to make it even larger. When he was finished, the cabin and the acreage it sat on were going to be Eric's home.

The unmarked road was little traveled and, with the exception of the people who owned the other cabins along the lake, traffic was rare. The road twisted and turned, giving the properties even more privacy as it took the residents further into the countryside, which was as scenic as it was reclusive. As Eric's truck wound around a curve, he noticed a car pulled up into the cabin to the north of his grandfather's property. That's funny, he thought. I've been staying here for a couple months and have never seen anyone there before.

On a whim, Eric turned into the gravel driveway. As he neared the cabin, he noticed an elderly man sitting on the front porch, who quickly rose to greet him.

"Hi, there," he said. "Eric Schultz—I'm staying in the cabin just down the road. I haven't seen you here before, so I thought I'd swing by and introduce myself."

"Good to meet you, young man," the gentleman said. "The name's Carl—Carl Vaughn."

"It's great to have a neighbor. I've often wondered who lived here—do you live here? Or is this your summer cabin?"

"Well, I guess you could say it's like a summer cabin. Actually my friends and I have been coming here to hunt and fish for many years. It's going to be sad to the see the place go, but it's time," Carl explained.

"Oh, are you going to sell the cabin?"

"Well, I don't think there's all that much to sell. The cabin itself hasn't been updated since I bought it 40 years ago. It's probably not worth anything to anyone, except myself. So I figured I'd knock it down and sell the land. It's a nice piece of property, and I'm sure some young person like yourself could build something nice here and start anew."

"Tear it down?" Eric asked, shocked. "But these old wood cabins are historic. They belong here. Besides, they don't make them like this anymore. As a matter of fact, I'm adding on to my grandfather's cabin and want to keep it as authentic as possible, but there's no way I can match the old logs and stones. The old wood floors are in decent shape, but some boards are rotted. If I could save them, I would. But it's not looking good. There are just so few places like these old cabins anymore."

"I admire your passion, son," the old man said. "But the place is getting to be an eyesore. Besides, I just don't have a use for it anymore. Unfortunately, a couple members of the old gang have passed on. The rest of the fellas have retired and settled down. Over the years, we've come here less and less. We haven't hunted the land in years, although last year we threw a hook and a line in a time or two. In reality, the last time we all got together it was mostly for sentimental reasons—a trip down memory lane, so to speak."

"Mr. Vaughn, I'd hate to see the cabin get torn down. I'm a builder—a craftsman in the construction trade—and I could help you get this place fixed up if you'd like," Eric offered.

Carl stood and opened the door. "Please, come in. Let's get out of the sun and talk."

They sat at the kitchen table, and Carl poured them each a glass of iced tea.

"I'd like to thank you for your offer," Carl said. "But I want to get the property ready to sell. You see, I recently sold my business, and my wife and I are relocating. It's time to enjoy our time together and spend it with our grandchildren. I will admit, though, that I'm going to miss this old cabin," he said, looking around. "Oh, if these walls could talk."

"Oh, yeah? I take it you and your friends had some good times here," Eric replied.

"Yes. Good times, indeed. You see, this place wasn't just a fishing cabin. It wasn't just any old cabin—it was the people in the cabin that made it what it was. We hunted here, we fished here, and we made plans here. Big plans, mighty big plans."

"What kinds of plans?" Eric asked.

"You name it, we planned it. Businesses were born here, son. Ideas became multimillion dollar inventions. At times, there was more motivation, inspiration, and debate in this room than there was when the Cubs finally made it to the World Series. Eric, while most guys leave a fishing trip with tall tales about the big one that got away, we left this cabin with tall goals that we never let go of. Oh, if these walls could talk, the tales they would tell ... "

"Wow. I'm really impressed," Eric said, looking around the cabin. "Now that I know that, it seems even more of a shame to tear this cabin down. It seems like you'd want to preserve some of its history and all those memories."

"Oh, those memories are preserved, I assure you. They're now on store shelves. They're features in automobiles. They're part of technology and medicine. It wasn't the cabin that inspired them—it was the great minds that visited here, all working in synergy to support and advise each other. We were quite a team, young man, quite a team."

Eric paused, letting his new friend reminisce for a moment. Then, he got an idea.

"Um, Mr. Vaughn, excuse me, but I'd like to make you an offer."

"You want to buy this cabin?"

"Oh, no. I'm sorry. Um, actually, I was thinking that I would be happy to tear it down for you—for free. You'd get what you want and it wouldn't cost you a dime. The only thing I'd ask is that you let me keep and preserve as much of it as possible. I'd love to incorporate the history of this cabin into my cabin. I could use some of the materials, and I assure you, I'd take great pride in knowing that I was able to preserve such an important piece of your past."

"Hmmm. Well, that is something to think about. I can certainly afford to pay someone to take the cabin off my hands, but if you're serious, I'd actually prefer to let you knock it down, and I think the fellas would agree. I came here this weekend to remove some of the items I want to keep, but I was going to leave other furnishings and items behind. If they are of any interest to you, you're welcome to anything you can use," Carl offered.

"Thank you, sir. Thank you so much," Eric said, shaking the gentleman's hand. "I promise I'll get to work on it as soon as you're ready, and I'll clean the site up when I'm done. It will be all ready to go on the market. Just let me know when I can get started."

Eric jotted down his name and phone number on a notepad he found sitting in the center of the table, grateful that he'd followed his instincts and stopped by to introduce himself. The materials from the cabin could be repurposed for the addition and would fit in with his grandfather's cabin quite well. That made Eric think of something.

"Hey, Mr. Vaughn, since you've been here so long, did you know my grandfather, William Schultz? Since your properties are side by side, had you two ever met?"

"Oh, yes, young man. I did know your grandfather. I only saw him once every few months, for a couple days at a time, but, yes, we knew each other. As a matter of fact, back in the day, we hunted and fished a time or two. Your grandfather had a great mind, Eric. I admired William very much, and he spoke highly of you, though I'm sure you were a young lad back then."

Smiling, Eric chuckled. "I'm sure I was. Thank you. That means so much to me," Eric said. "I'll leave you alone now. Just give me a call about when I can start. In the meantime, if you need anything, I'm just down the road."

* * *

Watching Eric's truck back out of the driveway, Carl thought about what had transpired. Although he'd just met the young man, he liked him. In fact, there was something about Eric that reminded him very much of William, who had been a good friend and neighbor whenever Carl had visited the cabin. Eventually, William even became a member of the mastermind group that had met in Carl Vaughn's cabin for decades. It was a closed group—a secret group in many ways—and most people believed they were just a group of guys who got together for a man cave kind of weekend. But it was more—so much more.

It's too bad, Carl thought, these walls can't talk. It was a shame that the secrets to their successes couldn't be passed on, especially to Eric. William would have liked that ....

Then Carl had an idea. Pulling his keys out of his pocket, he went to the old desk under the living room window and unlocked the center drawer. Reaching in, he pulled out a metal box and set it on the table in front of him. With one turn of the key it opened, and Carl reached in and picked up a handful of tokens.

Maybe, just maybe, these walls can talk, he thought, smiling.

Chapter 2

Dreams of Business

The next morning, Eric sat down with coffee to plan his week. He expected to finish the addition to the Bradford house before the end of the week, but he didn't have any major projects lined up after that. With the exception of a few small jobs that often were passed on to him by larger general contractors, business was slow. Looking for work wasn't new to him, but it wasn't something he enjoyed having to do.

He'd always loved building things and had started at a young age. From birdhouses to porch benches, he had developed his craft. When he got out of high school, he became an apprentice for a builder and worked on actual homes. The end product was always a source of pride for him, and he knew this was what he wanted to do with his life.

However, Eric wanted to own his very own company. He didn't want to work for someone else, like his father had all of his life. He wanted to be more like his grandfather, who had been a successful business owner. Eric always admired his grandfather's lifestyle and often wished his father had followed in those footsteps, instead of punching a time clock without any real chance of getting ahead. The security and stability that would come from owning his own business enticed him to become an independent contractor.

He'd always been a hard worker and someone who took pride in doing a good job. He was a stickler for details and always strove for perfection. But after eight years in the business, Eric still struggled to compete with large contractors. He simply didn't have the crew to take on big projects, but he knew that until his business grew, he couldn't keep a crew working or afford to pay them.

Eric was aware that part of his problem was a lack of business acumen. He was a master craftsman, but he simply didn't have the business background to grow from a one-man operation into a successful and busy general contractor. It would be nice if Grandpa was here, he thought. Then I'd have someone to turn to for advice.

His grandfather had always been a role model and mentor. Whenever they spent time together, he shared his wisdom with Eric. "Work smarter, not harder," he'd say. "Don't be afraid to take risks and learn something new. Be willing to ask for advice."

The list went on. When Eric's grandfather offered advice, Eric listened. But he had been young and, while he admired his grandfather deeply, he just wasn't ready for the lessons at the time.

But now he was and he wished he'd paid more attention. His grandfather had experience and knew how to grow a business and build a customer base. Eric was certain that he could have turned to him and learned what he needed to do to become a successful business owner. With a sigh, he resigned himself to the fact that he'd just have to figure it out for himself. Hopefully, he'd be able to do that before circumstances forced him to resort to working for someone else.

* * *

After lunch, Eric went to work on the cabin. At least he wouldn't have to replace all the flooring, he thought. If Carl let him take what he wanted before the cabin was torn down, he'd be able to replace the areas of the floor that were irreparable with salvaged boards. After sanding them down and refinishing them, they'd be a perfect match and no one would ever know they weren't original to the existing structure.

First, though, he needed to upgrade the electricity and plumbing, which weren't up to code. He'd just begun to replace the pipes behind the shower wall when the phone rang.

"Hello," he answered.

"Eric, it's Carl Vaughn. How are you today?"

"Good. And you?"

"Fine thank you. As a matter of fact, I think I've gotten everything done here and I've packed everything

I need to take with me. So you can start taking anything you need tomorrow, if you're ready."

"Oh, so soon?" Eric replied. "Well, good—I will try to work quickly. And, sir, thank you again. I really appreciate your kindness."

"The pleasure is mine, son. But there is one thing I ask in return."

"What's that?"

"I've left an envelope here for you, where you will find my contact information, as well as a little gift from me for volunteering to demolish this old place. Let's just call it a token of my appreciation. Oh, and you'll also find a note from me with a bit of, shall we say, instruction on what I'd like you to do," Carl said.

"Thank you so much," Eric said. "But you didn't have to do anything or give me anything. Letting me use what I can from the cabin is payment enough."

"Consider it a gift. Just promise that you will use it wisely," the old man replied.

"I can promise that. I will stop by tomorrow after work and get started. Will you be there?"

"No. I'll be leaving here shortly, but I'll leave the key under the mat. I'd like you to keep me up to date on your progress and let me know if you need anything. Take your time, though, there's no big rush to sell the land. It's not going anywhere," he laughed.

After they hung up, Eric thought about their conversation. It was mighty generous of the old man to let him take anything he wanted out of the cabin, but he'd also left something for him—a token of appreciation. It was a thoughtful gesture, but one that left Eric more than curious about what it might be. He figured he'd just have to wait until tomorrow to find out. Picking up his pipe wrench, he went back into the bathroom.

* * *

Eric made great progress on the addition he'd been working on, and it looked like the job would be finished on time. He'd spent the day hanging the drywall and getting it taped. Tomorrow it would be ready to mud and sand. Satisfied that he'd done as much as he could, he packed up his tools and headed home, remembering that he first had to stop at Carl's cabin as he'd promised.

Even though Eric knew no one was home, he knocked before hunting for the key and opening the door. True to his word, Carl hadn't taken much. He'd left behind the kitchen table and a couple chairs. The old desk still sat in the corner, but it looked like all the personal items had been removed. There were no pictures or mail lying around as far as he could see. Eric would make sure he talked to Carl to see if he was coming back for anything or would like the things he had left behind put in storage.

On the table sat an envelope with his name written in large letters across the front. Sitting in one of the chairs, Eric picked it up and broke the seal. Reaching in, he pulled out a sheet of paper.

Eric,

Years ago, this cabin was the meeting place for some of the best business minds I've ever known. Your grandfather was one of them. Our meetings were by invitation only and there was an entry fee: every time a successful business owner joined us, he would be asked to trade one of his success tips for every prize trophy he bagged. Over the years, we accumulated quite a few prize trophies—the fish and game here were as plentiful as the business discussions, I assure you.

I promised that you could have anything in this cabin. The collective knowledge of your grandfather and the other members of our little club, shall we say, is more valuable than anything else that is or was in this cabin. So I want to pass it on to you. In this envelope you will find one of those tips, each of which were engraved on wooden tokens. I chose this one specifically for you because your grandfather, who had a bright mind and was generous about sharing his knowledge, contributed it. He would have wanted you to have it.

All I ask, Eric, is that you use this business tip wisely—learn about it and apply it to your business and your life. When you feel you have done that, send me a note or an email telling me what this tip means to you and how it has impacted your business.

I am certain that this is but the first of many communications we will enjoy. Thank you for allowing

me the opportunity to revisit the past and contribute to
your future.

Your friend,

Carl Vaughn

Intrigued, Eric reached his hand deep into the bottom of the envelope, and his fingers found their prize—a round wooden token. He pulled it out and read the one word engraved into it: *Illuminate.*

According to Carl, this was supposed to be a business success tip, but Eric had no idea what it meant. But he was willing to do whatever it took to find out.

Chapter 3

Illuminate

Monday morning, Eric woke early. He didn't need an alarm clock; the birds chirping outside did the trick—and there were plenty of them around the cabin. It was, after all, built to correlate with the wildlife and the surroundings.

Showered and dressed, he hopped in his truck and set out to the job site, but first he needed to stop at the coffee shop and get his usual: a large coffee, one cream, no sugar. As usual, the shop was busy with regulars—mostly guys like him stopping in to grab coffee and a breakfast sandwich or donut. He whipped his truck into a parking spot next to a much newer truck with a professional logo he recognized. *Must be the crew building the apartment complex across the street,* he thought, knowing they had a fleet of work trucks, a perk they were able to offer their employees.

"Hey, Joe," he said, recognizing a carpenter who he'd gotten to know enough to speak to whenever they saw each other. "How's it going?"

"Can't complain. And you? How's business treating you? Staying busy?"

"Yeah, finishing up an addition this week. If you hear of anything, though, I'd appreciate it if you'd let me know."

"Will do, Eric," Joe replied. It was a courtesy his company sometimes extended. After all, the company was working on a big project, one that would take months to complete. They didn't have the time to mess with smaller jobs and were happy to pass them on to smaller businesses like Eric's that weren't a threat to their customer base.

After stirring his coffee, Eric walked to the counter and paid for it. Deciding not to splurge on breakfast, he thanked the cashier and walked out the door.

"Hey, Eric!"

Seeing Joe standing next to his truck, Eric walked over.

"I almost forgot—some of the fellas and I are going to stop at Smitty's Wednesday night to watch the game. You're welcome to join us if you'd like."

"Wednesday? Sure, I'll try to make it. Thanks for asking me," Eric replied.

"All right. See ya then!" Joe said before climbing into his truck and taking off.

Thinking that it would be nice to get out of the house and hang out with the guys for a change, Eric drove to the job site. The shingles were strategically placed across the roof, ready to begin. Suddenly, Eric was glad he had lined up a couple of helpers—roofing was hard work, especially when the afternoon sun was beating down. Sure, their wages would dip into his profits, but this was one time when it was worth it.

Inside, he busied himself with mudding the drywall, hoping to make some headway before his workers came. They were two brothers, neither of whom had a full-time job. However, they were happy with side jobs—whenever they needed a few bucks, they got the word out that they were looking for work. Eric had worked with them before and liked them. They did good work; they just lacked ambition.

Thinking about that reminded him of the token, which at the last minute this morning he had slipped into his pocket. Illuminate. He really wished he knew what that meant—he didn't have a clue what Carl and his buddies were referring to. Pulling out the token, he looked at it quickly before climbing up the ladder. Maybe it will just come to me, he thought.

The day passed quickly, just as it always does when you're busy. His helpers actually had to point out to him that it was quitting time. Looking at his phone, he saw that it was five o'clock on the dot. *They are punctual, yes—ambitious, no*, Eric thought with a smile.

"Thanks a lot, guys," he said. "We're just about done, so I can take it from here. I'll stop by and pay you after I run to the bank."

Packing his tools, he secured the job site and headed to the nearest bank branch to cash a check. He was feeling productive and proud of a good honest day's work, until he saw the balance in his checkbook—a reminder that even taking pride in doing a good job was sometimes not enough.

I need to get serious about figuring out how to boost my business. Maybe Carl and Grandpa's business gurus can help, if I put my mind to it.

The token in his pocket was nagging at him. Illuminate. Maybe that meant he needed to advertise and promote his business better, kind of like Joe's company with their big white trucks and bright red logos. Anyone who drove past them could identify who they worked for.

But Eric knew that was a catch-22. He couldn't afford those trucks and that kind of marketing until he started getting more work and bringing in more money. Again, he let the thought slide, hoping he'd somehow figure out this business tip and how it applied to him.

* * *

Eric spent the next two days sanding the drywall and finishing the roof. On Thursday, he'd clean up and make his final inspection, ensuring that no detail had been overlooked. Standing back, he admired his work, knowing that the homeowner would be happy with it, too.

At the last minute, he almost decided not to join Joe and the guys at Smitty's but then figured it might be a good idea. They all talked shop when they got together, and it might be a good way for him to pick up some leads on work. His calendar was wide open starting Friday.

Showered and changed, he walked into the neighborhood sports bar, where he spotted Joe and a few others sitting at a table and surrounded by wall-to-wall televisions.

"Hey, guys," he said, reaching out to shake hands.

"Glad you made it, Eric. Sit down," one of them said, pulling a chair out.

The group joked with the table next to them while watching the game for a while before talk turned to work.

"You got anything lined up yet, Eric?" Joe asked.

"No, not yet. I just wish I could figure out how to keep the work flowing without breaks. Don't get me wrong; something will come up—it always does. It would be nice to keep it steady, though. How do you guys always manage to have work?"

"Hey don't look at me—I don't get the jobs. I just do them. The guy you need to talk to is—hey, Saul, come here, will you?" he yelled across to the next table. "Eric here has something to ask you."

"Oh no, that's not necessary," Eric said, but his argument was futile. Joe's boss, Saul, was already headed to their table.

"'Talk to Saul—he loves to talk business. I swear that's what he'd do 24/7 if he could," Joe laughed. "Here, he can have my seat—I'm going to go grab a sandwich."

"Hello, Eric. Joe said you have a question. How can I help you?"

"Well, it's really nothing. I was just talking to Joe and complaining about not having work lined up. I didn't mean for him to bother you," Eric said.

"It's not a bother at all. So what's the problem?"

"I don't know, really. I try to do my best, and my customers say they're very happy with my work. But it's a struggle to get the next job lined up. And then I usually have to reduce my costs or fees to be the low bid. I don't get it—my customers are happy. I always try to meet every deadline, and I do good work. I thought if you worked hard, took pride in your work, and aimed to please, the business would come. But after eight years, nothing has changed."

"Hmmm, well, Eric, I think you're on to something," Saul said.

"I am? Good! Tell me what it is, please."

"You're telling me everything that you're doing right. And that's all good. But there are a lot of construction companies, and I hope most of them are doing things right, too. That means that you're no different than them ... and you still haven't figured out what the problem is."

"Bingo. How can I do that?"

"Listen to what I said. You haven't figured out what the *problem* is. Eric, you're focusing on everything that you're doing right, but if you want to find out why your business isn't growing, you should be doing the opposite—focusing on what you're not doing right."

"Huh? I don't get it," Eric said, confused.

"You know what you're doing right, son. That part is easy. But if you want to grow your business, you have to figure out why you're not getting the business. You already know why people want to hire you. Now you have to figure out why they aren't. Shine some light on that and you'll have your answer."

It was an aha moment. Like a light bulb going on in his head, Eric got it. Illuminate! Carl and his rich friends weren't talking about billboards or neon signs—they were referring to something mental. He'd been so worried about making sure everything was "right" with his work that he hadn't even entertained the idea that anything could be wrong. If he could discover what things were wrong, he would then be able to fix them.

"Do you have any idea what some of these problems might be?" he asked the older, wiser businessman.

"I've heard great things about your work, Eric. My guess is the problem doesn't have anything at all to do with what you do or how you do it. No, I'm willing to bet that the problem isn't in your talent or your skill. It's in your head. If you want your business to grow, you have to have the mind-set that allows it to happen. It's all about focusing on what you don't know, learning about it, and eliminating your obstacles."

"Illuminate," Eric said. "It means that I cannot grow until I figure out what's holding me back and addressing that first. It's kind of like the saying 'what you don't know can't hurt you,' but in reality, what you don't know can hurt you!"

Excited, Eric quickly threw a tip on the table, shook Saul's hand and thanked him profusely, and waved goodbye to Joe. He was in a hurry to get home and do some research on his laptop.

It was time to shed some light and focus on what was holding him back. Only then would he be able to move past it and build a business his grandfather would have been proud of.

And when he was done, he had an email to write to his friend, Carl Vaughn.

Chapter 4

Confidence

That night, Eric emailed Carl Vaughn, letting him know that the first token he'd received was, indeed, opening his eyes and broadening his perspective. He mentioned that he wasn't quite sure where this illumination process would take him, but was excited to see what it would expose and how he could use the information to build his business.

He spent the next day at Carl's cabin, pulling down some ceiling beams and floorboards that were in great shape. He was certain that he could integrate the pieces into his cabin in such a way that they no one would be able to tell they hadn't been there since day one. It was part of the challenge and the beauty of what he did, making each construction project look as if no detail had been overlooked.

As the day wound down, he walked back the narrow lane to his mailbox. Thumbing through his mail at home, he separated the junk mail from his bills, one of which caught his eye. It was a recurring bill for an ad he'd been running in a construction industry newsletter for the last year or so. Without thinking, he automatically reached in his pocket for his checkbook to pay the next installment, but then he hesitated.

Hmm, I wonder if I'm getting any return from this investment.

Eric contemplated the answer to that question. Had he received any business from placing an ad in this publication? And if so, did it justify the cost?

Each question seemed to spur another, and Eric knew precisely what he had to do—illuminate. He had to find out what wasn't working before he could focus solely on what was working. Grabbing a pen and pad of paper, he listed all of the new clients he'd taken on since he'd run the ad.

What he learned was enlightening. He always asked new clients how they got his name, and none of them had mentioned the ad. It was quite telling. For one thing, he was advertising in a construction magazine, a publication homeowners weren't likely to see. And all of his clients had told him that they'd gotten his name from people they knew, who had hired him in the past.

All of his new clients had come from referrals, and any other jobs were from repeat customers who had been happy with his work. He'd had this information all along but had faithfully renewed his ad, hoping that it would attract clientele. And it hadn't.

He wondered what to do with this information—obviously, the advertisement wasn't in his best interest, but what was? If referrals were his most effective method of marketing, how could he get more?

Then it hit him! What if he used the money he'd been spending on the ad to give his clients an incentive to refer him to their friends and relatives? It didn't have to be a lot—maybe $50 for each referral—but it would be a good way to show his appreciation for their loyalty and support, and it just might bring him a few more clients.

Grabbing a pen, he wrote the word "Cancel" across the invoice and inserted it in the prepaid envelope that accompanied it. Then he made a list of all of the clients he'd had in the past several years before sitting down at the computer and writing a letter thanking them for their past business. To express his gratitude, he included an offer of $50 for every referral that became a new client.

It was a new marketing tactic, but Eric felt good about it. There was absolutely no risk, with a probable likelihood of gain, at least more so than running a blind ad that had never produced results.

He printed out his letters, signing each one and hand addressing the envelopes. It was a personal touch he hoped would resonate with his clients. At the very least, they'd be less likely to assume it was junk mail and throw it aside. Admiring his stack of envelopes, he placed them on the table next to the front door so he would remember to take them to the post office.

The next morning, Eric made his coffee and checked his email, surprised to see that Carl had replied.

Eric,

I am pleased that you are shedding light on your first token! I specifically chose Illuminate because it is a process, not just a step, and it can and should be used when you are using the principles addressed in future tokens. You see, in every business strategy or philosophy, we must not only determine what is working, but we must also focus on what isn't working well so it can be fixed. Problems do not go away when they are swept under the rug. Oftentimes, they become larger. By shedding light on them, though, you will be able to address issues before they negatively impact your business.

That said, you will find your next token in a likely spot—under the rug on the front porch!

Your friend,

Carl

After taking his letters to the post office, Eric made the return trip to the cabin, stopping first to get his next token. It was like a scavenger hunt, and Eric was finding that the game was fun. He lifted the mat at the front door, where true to his word, Carl had left one wooden token. Picking it up, Eric rubbed his thumb across it, exposing one word: *Confidence.*

Confidence? Eric had always felt confident, so he wasn't sure how this token applied to him. He had never doubted his skills or his abilities. As a matter of fact, he took pride in them. Maybe this token was a fluke and didn't relate to him, he thought, sliding it into his pocket.

That afternoon, Eric realized he was running low on supplies, so he made another trip to the hardware store. Even though he wasn't a commercial or industrial contractor, he was a vendor, so he had a running business account at the store and was known by the employees, who were always more than helpful and friendly.

"Hey, Eric. How's it going? The cabin coming along okay?" asked Gene, the assistant manager.

"It's coming along, slowly but surely," Eric replied. "Actually, I'm about ready to strip and refinish some floorboards. So I'll need to rent your industrial sander and buffer."

"Well, you are moving along. Let me know when you're finished—I'd like to swing by and see what you've done with it."

"Will do, Gene. Now, how much is it to rent the sander? I'm guessing I'll need it for two days."

"It's not cheap. Actually, Eric, you're better off buying a new one outright. As a contractor, you get a discount, and rental fees are pretty high. If you think you'll ever use it again, I suggest you buy it. It'll pay for itself after just two or three jobs."

"Hmm. I wish I could buy it, Gene. But I think my credit limit is about maxed out, so I'm going to have to pass. But thanks, anyway."

"Sit down, Eric," Gene motioned to a chair near the counter. "From what I can see, you've carried the same credit limit since the day you opened your account here."

"Uh, that's right. I don't think I qualify for an increase—at least not until my business grows a little bit more."

"Well, that's where you might be wrong, Eric. You're automatically assuming that we will reject a request for a credit increase. That might not be the case. Actually, we want your business and try to work with our vendors every chance we get."

"I know, and I appreciate it. But I'm pretty sure that I won't qualify for a credit increase. So I think I'll save myself the embarrassment,"

"Eric, you don't have to be embarrassed. First, you have paid your monthly invoice on time every month for three years. That's a great track record and the kind of vendor we want to do business with. Have a little confidence—it can't hurt to try. And who knows? A credit increase could help your cash flow quite a bit—and it can save you money on things like this industrial sander."

A bell went off in Eric's head—confidence. Maybe confidence was an issue. What if Gene was right and he qualified for a credit increase, but was afraid to ask for it so he didn't have to risk rejection? What if they said no? But what if he applied and they said yes?

"You know what, Gene, I'd like to sleep on it. So I'll just grab the hardware I need and I'll get back to you about the sander, if that's okay," Eric said.

"Sure—but I'd really like you to think about it, Eric. I believe we can help you."

* * *

The conversation was still replaying in his head when he went home. Unable to make a decision, he decided to email his friend, Carl.

Carl,

I found the next token, confidence. At first, I didn't think it pertained to me. After all, I'm quite confident with my work. However, an incident at the hardware store today weighs on me. I was asked if I wanted to apply for a credit increase; however, I am struggling to maintain a steady flow of projects. I'm almost maxed out on my credit line as it is. For the first time, it's come to my attention that I might not be as confident about some things as I thought.

What are your thoughts?

Eric

Carl replied that very evening.

Eric,

Every business owner has had their confidence tested at some time. Usually, that confidence relates to something other than products or services. Confidence is a much broader concept, son. You can have the most amazing idea, invention or skill, but without confidence, you'll never be able to convince others of its worth. Without confidence, you'll never be able to attract investors. Without confidence, you'll never be able to keep up with the competition.

Knowing that, Eric, can you honestly say that you believe you are confident?

Your friend,

Carl

Eric pondered those questions and realized that Carl was right. Eric did lack confidence in those areas, especially when it came to financial matters or competing with bigger contractors. He couldn't imagine himself asking an investor for funding, much less convincing an investor that it would be a good idea. When it came to competition, Eric admitted that he bowed out and avoided competing with bigger contractors to save himself rejection, embarrassment … but most of all, disappointment.

Am I keeping myself small by refusing to grow my business? I'm reluctant to ask for a credit increase, and I avoid big jobs because I'm certain that I won't get them. What could happen if I had the confidence to sell myself and my business?

Before he lost the nerve, he logged onto his computer to find out.

The first order of business was to apply for a credit increase with the building supply store.

His phone rang at 7:00 a.m. the next morning.

"Eric, it's Gene from Builder's Supply Inc. I thought I'd personally call and give you the news. After reviewing your application and your strong payment history, we've doubled your credit limit. I'm so glad you decided to give it a try—maybe you should have done it a long time ago."

"No, kidding! That's great. But I'm actually surprised," Eric replied.

"Well, I'm not—I was confident you'd be approved all along. A little belief goes a long way. Now, when do you want to come in and sign the papers?"

"How about this morning when I come in to pick up my new industrial floor sander?" Eric laughed. "And, Gene, I want to thank you for believing in me when I didn't believe in myself."

"No problem, buddy. Let this win boost your confidence so next time you won't let an opportunity pass you by. If you don't try, you can't win."

Chapter 5

Integrity

After working on refinishing his cabin's hardwood floors, Eric was ready for a break. Grabbing his fishing pole and tackle box, he went out the back door. There was nothing more peaceful to him than sitting by the lake and enjoying nature's beauty. Fishing was merely an excuse to do that—after all, most of the time, he didn't catch anything—and when he did, he usually threw it back.

His thoughts wandered as he imagined his grandfather sitting on this very spot, under the shade of a gnarly old oak tree. It was the same spot where his grandfather had taught him to fish when he was just a boy. A couple decades later, he wished he'd heeded the words that his grandpa had generously shared and remembered the tales of the older man's adventures.

Most of all, he wished his grandfather was around to answer his questions and pass along some advice.

A sudden bend of his fishing pole brought him back to the present. There was always something thrilling about the catch, reeling it in, and taking pride in the sport. Today was no different. He yanked the pole back and reeled the line in a few times, pausing just enough to relax the fish before repeating the process and bringing it closer. Before he was able to reel it to shore, though, he lost resistance in the line.

"Oh, the one that got away."

Eric turned around to find his friend, Kevin, standing behind him with a big grin on his face.

"It was a big one, I tell ya," Eric laughed. "Good to see you. It's been a while. What's up?"

"Ah, not much. Deb's at her parents' house tonight, so I thought I'd stop by and see how the cabin's coming along."

"It's coming. I'm not in a big hurry, as you can see. But I'm making progress, slowly but surely."

"Great. Hey, you been busy? Do you have a lot of work lined up?"

"No, nothing at the moment, but I do have feelers out. Actually, I'm trying something different and giving former clients a fee for referrals. It's an experiment, I guess, but I hope something pans out."

"Eric, you do excellent work … and speaking of referrals, that's another reason I stopped by. My in-laws are getting their house ready to sell. That's why Deb's there right now, helping them go through decades of stuff they've accumulated. Anyway, I thought I'd give you a heads up—they're going to downsize, but they want to build. I told them to give you a call. You up for it?"

"You bet I am! When are they ready to start? How do I get a hold of them? Oh, and hey, I'll make sure you get a referral fee!"

"Slow down, buddy. First, I gave them your number, and they said they're going to call you this week. And you don't have to give me that referral fee. I mean, what are friends for?"

"I appreciate it. I really do. You know, as a general contractor, I'll have to hire subcontractors—it's a big step for me—one that could make a huge difference."

"I know. But I have faith in you, Eric. I wouldn't have recommended you if I didn't. Now, how about a tour of your homestead?"

After walking Kevin through the cabin and telling him about his plans to update the kitchen, while retaining its vintage rustic style, Eric was disappointed that Kevin had to leave. It was always good to see him, but since Kevin and Debbie had become an item, they didn't get together very often.

After promising to keep in touch, Eric walked down the lane to check his mailbox, surprised to see an envelope with the old man's handwriting on it. Feeling the contents, he knew right away that it contained another token.

Eric,

There are many things you can do to improve their business, but it's just as important, if not more so, to focus on your characteristics, for they will dictate your success more than anything. Integrity matters.

Your friend,

Carl

Reaching in, he pulled out the wooden token that was inscribed with the word *Integrity* on one side and *Ethics* on the other.

Interesting, he thought. I just wonder how it applies to me.

Two days later, Debbie's father called him, and they scheduled an appointment for the next day. After looking over the house plans, Eric made a few recommendations—changes that he thought would improve the layout and one that would save the couple a few thousand dollars. Eric took the plans home, promising to prepare a bid and get it back to them in a couple days.

It was a job that Eric really wanted, so he tried to figure out ways to reduce his bid to ensure he'd be awarded the project. He could try to cut labor costs, but he was reminded of something his father had said. "Eric, you should always hire the best you can afford, not the cheapest you can get."

To Eric, that also meant he couldn't cut corners on the quality of the materials. That's where reputations took a big hit, and his reputation was something he was trying to build, not destroy. In the end, he decided to prepare the bid as realistically as possible, using the acceptable pay scale for the trades and allowing for a reasonable profit for himself. It was an honest bid, and all he could do was hope for the best.

He delivered the bid two days later as promised. To his surprise, Debbie's father took one look at the final figure and said, "You're hired. When can you get started?'

Eric had been prepared to discuss the bid and how he came to his numbers, justifying them if he needed to. "Are you sure? You don't want to review the bid?"

"No. I trust Kevin. If he says you're my man, that's good enough for me. How about we take a ride to the lot?"

Eric liked what he saw—the lot was clear with the exception of a few established trees that didn't have to be cut down. It was in a newer residential neighborhood, and the houses were all single-family dwellings with attached garages on half-acre lots. Eric was happy to know he'd be the builder for at least one of them.

He was happy to tell his friend, Carl, about it in his next email.

"This project has the potential to be really good for my business. At first, I thought I'd have to find a way to cut costs to get the bid, but that wasn't the case. And I have to admit, I'm reluctant to reduce quality when it comes to my work and customers. I guess that's what integrity is about. Right?

"Oh, I almost forgot to mention that I got the job through a referral. And my friend says he doesn't want the referral fee! Win!"

Carl's reply wasn't quite what he expected.

Eric,

Integrity is more than quality. It's about saying what you'll do and doing what you say. No matter what. Think about it.
Carl

Eric fully intended to build the house according to specs, giving the customer precisely what he wanted and nothing less, leaving him to wonder just what Carl was referring to. Then it hit him—he promised a fee when he got a project from a referral, and that promise didn't change because Kevin had generously refused it. Integrity—his word was his promise, not only to his customers, but to himself. He had to be a man of his word and honor his promises, even if other people didn't expect him to.

Ultimately, the one person he had to answer to was himself. It was about being true to his word and a person others could trust. That was integrity. It was, in fact, a principle that his grandfather had lived by. And he knew in his heart that his grandfather would never have backed down from a commitment or a promise, no matter how small.

Carl was right. Kevin might not care about a $50 referral fee, but Eric did. Sure, he could save himself a few dollars by letting it slide, but he knew now that it would bother him if he didn't follow through. Writing out a check and a thank-you note to his friend, he put the envelope on the table so he'd remember to mail it the next day. Even though his bank account was a little lighter, he felt good about it.

I guess there are things money can't buy, and pride is one of them, he thought.

Chapter 6

Optimism

Eric had the house plans in hand. Actually, they were spread across his kitchen table, where he had spent hours going over them to make sure he was ready to proceed with the project. There was a lot of planning that went into building a house, and he found himself a little overwhelmed. Poor planning would result in down time and project delays—the trades would be waiting for one thing to be completed before taking over. Keeping the project moving at a consistent and steady pace was part of Eric's job.

The excavators were breaking ground in two weeks, and Eric was lining up his subcontractors. They'd need plumbers and pipefitters, electricians, masons and bricklayers, roofers, drywallers, and carpenters ... and that was before the flooring could be installed and the painters could move in. And Eric had to coordinate every step of the process.

In addition to keeping the project moving smoothly, Eric had to make sure the supplies got to the construction site by the time the trades were ready for them. On top of that, he had to make sure they were all paid.

Caught up in the excitement of overseeing this construction, Eric hadn't considered the fact that he would assume so much responsibility. If anything went wrong, it could affect his reputation among his peers in the industry and with homeowners. He suddenly got a case of the "What-ifs?" What if the weather didn't cooperate? What if there were delays due to poor scheduling? What if materials weren't delivered when needed? What if his subcontractors weren't reliable?

What if I fail?

Walking away from the table, he picked up the phone, hoping his friend Carl was available.

Carl answered on the second ring and listened patiently while Eric explained his predicament.

"I thought I was confident, but I guess I'm not."

"Oh, you are confident. You know you are detailed and follow through. You knew you were ready to take your business to the next level. Confidence isn't your problem, Eric. You're being pessimistic—thinking that whatever can go wrong will go wrong. Being an optimist is a necessary characteristic for success, son. I was actually saving that token for later, but it seems like you need it now. I'll put it in the mail to you, along with the next token that I think will come in handy."

"Optimistic?"

"Yes, believe me, every entrepreneur will attest to the fact that without *optimism*, you will never know what you can do. In fact, you won't even try."

"But how do I become more optimistic?"

"Do your homework, son. You'll figure it out. And when you do, let me know."

Eric hung up the phone more confused than before. What kind of homework or research could he do to learn more about being optimistic?

Then it dawned on him. Grabbing his truck keys, he drove across town to talk to the one person who would have the answer. She always did.

"Hi, Mom!" he yelled as he walked through the kitchen door.

"Oh, Eric! It's so good to see you," she said after giving him a big hug. "Are you hungry?"

Good old mom, always ready to make sure her boys were properly fed.

"Well, actually, I could use some home cooking. Got enough for me to stay for supper?"

"Always. Now, what brings you by? You're so busy working on the cabin we don't see you much anymore … and your dad told me that you're going to be building a new house for Kevin's in-laws. I'm proud of you."

"Well, thanks. But that's one reason I stopped by. Do you remember when I was a kid and hated doing my homework?" Eric asked.

"Boy, do I. You hated science so much that you

wouldn't even try it. You used to argue that you were going to get it wrong, anyway, so what was the use?" she replied.

"Do you remember what I used to tell you, Eric?" she asked then, pausing for his answer.

"Whether you think can or you think you can't, you're right," he spouted from memory.

"It's true. If you don't think you can do something, you're not going to try very hard. But when you think you can do something, it's not so tough and you jump right in and get it done."

"So it's all in my mind," Eric mused.

"It's just like when you had to learn to tie your shoes before you went to kindergarten. Oh, how we struggled. And every time, after a couple tries, you'd give up. But when push came to shove, you had to decide what was most important to you—going to kindergarten or refusing to learn how to tie your shoelaces."

"I remember! I remember how happy I was when I finally got it right."

"Oh, if I had a dime for every time you told me you couldn't do it … and another dime for every time I told you that you could do it. You just had to try."

"Yes! And, Mom, I remember how you got me to learn. It seemed so complicated and confusing, but you told me that I could accomplish anything if I just broke it down into steps. So we practiced the bunny ears and loops over and over."

"The same was true for homework—remember how I always told you to do the hardest subject first, then the rest would be easy? So I made you do your science work first."

"I wish everything was so simple now," Eric sighed. "You see, I'm getting a little scared about assuming the responsibilities of a general contractor. There are so many things that can go wrong. And what if I find that I can't do it, after all?"

"Worrying is the biggest time killer there is. Eric, 99% of the things we worry about don't happen. You're being a pessimist, like your Uncle Rick. He always believed if anything could go wrong, it would. I swear that's why he never amounted to anything—he knew without a doubt that he wouldn't succeed, so he didn't even bother."

His mom poured him a glass of iced tea, then pointed at it.

"Eric, is this glass half full or half empty?"

"Ummm, both," he grinned, getting where she was going with this.

"Seriously, son, look at your business like this glass. Imagine you are Uncle Rick. You wouldn't even try to build your business because you'd be certain you'd fail. The glass is half empty and you think you're heading toward doom before you even get started. Right?"

"Right," Eric nodded.

"And if that happens, you'll never really know if you have what it takes. Pessimists fail to try, but here's the thing about optimists—they can be realistic and plan for challenges along the way, but they get excited about the opportunities and potential ahead. They don't say, "What if I fail?"—they know that they have what it takes. Their glass is already half full, and it's up to them to add successes one by one to fill it to the brim."

Eric smiled, knowing that he'd come to the right person. His mom had always been able to get him to see the sunny side of things.

"Thanks, Mom. I knew I could count on you. I just have one question though. Do you think I'm ready? Do you think I can do this and succeed?"

"Eric, as your mom, I will always believe in you. But this time, what I think doesn't count. What do you think? Do you think you can, or do you think you can't? Either way, you'll be right."

"Well, I know that I'll always regret it if I don't try."

'That's my boy," she said, leaning over to kiss his forehead. "Now, just do the hardest part first … "

"And the rest will come easy," Eric finished for her.

"So, what's the hardest part? Maybe I can help," she offered.

"I guess I got overwhelmed just planning the whole thing … and thinking about payroll. It's a big responsibility, and I haven't done it before," Eric admitted.

"That's what you'll tackle first. So put your payroll money aside in a business account so you won't touch it. Your grandpa used to do that—he had different accounts for different things. Then, lay out a plan, but don't panic if something changes … that's going to happen no matter what you do. Plans can change, sometimes for the better. Don't building plans change from time to time?"

"Sure they do—a lot."

"What do you do when that happens?"

"I go with the flow and adjust."

"So that's just you'll do if you have to change your plan—go with the flow and adjust. As the general contractor, people are going to be looking to you for guidance and reassurance. When you're optimistic that it will work out, they will be, too. Oh and here's the bonus—once you're established and you're business is steady, you can hire people to do the things that you don't like to do!"

"I like your attitude, Mom. When you're optimistic that everything will be fine, you make me feel that way, too," Eric smiled.

"That's good. Now, why don't you go see what your father is doing in the garage and let him know dinner will be ready in a few minutes," she replied.

* * *

When Eric returned to the cabin, he looked at the house plans once again. Just a short while ago, he didn't have any work lined up, and now here he was with the biggest project he'd ever been trusted with.

His glass was half full, and he fully intended to focus on what he could do—not what he was afraid he couldn't do.

Nothing had changed, except his attitude. Funny how that works, he thought. His grandfather had always told him he could do anything he set his mind to, but he suddenly remember that he'd always finished it with one phrase, "The only person who can stop you from succeeding is you."

For the first time, he truly understood his grandfather's words, which reminded him—he needed to thank Carl for passing along some much-needed wisdom when it was needed the most.

Chapter 7

Relationships

The following week, Eric woke at the crack of dawn and worked late into the day. Building a house took a lot of work, and being the general contractor meant it was up to him to make sure no detail was overlooked. From day one, he intended to be there to answer any questions or handle any crisis, large or small, during the process.

Eric had been so busy he'd totally forgotten about Carl and the tokens, until he stopped to get his mail on Wednesday evening and found an envelope from his friend. True to his word, it contained a token with the word *Optimism* inscribed on it, as well as another token—this one inscribed with the word *Relationships*.

Hmmm, he thought, I'm not sure this token applies to me. He had never encountered any issues with the people he worked with in the past. Then again, he'd never overseen a large project with many crews before. Thus far, though, there hadn't been any issues. His workers had all shown up on time and knew their jobs well enough that they didn't require micromanaging. They were professionals, and that was precisely why Eric had chosen each subcontractor. If corners had to be cut, it would never be in the quality of craftsmanship that went into the house.

It was a plus, too, that Eric had a good relationship with his subcontractors. Right away, he let them know that he was there to help them in any way he could. And he meant it. A bad relationship could not only make for a miserable day, but it could also have a real impact on the effort put forth by the crews. He'd witnessed it before when one argument between a general contractor and a residential electrician had created tension amongst everyone on the job site. Sure, there were always going to be different ideas, personalities, and opinions, but Eric was committed to building both quality houses and relationships. Any disagreements needed to be addressed professionally and promptly, with respect for each party.

Shrugging, Eric tossed the token onto an end table, figuring he'd drop Carl a note later acknowledging receipt and thanking him for it. Actually, he was glad this wasn't something that he needed to learn about and address. He did make a mental note, though, to remember that the relationships on the job site were important and everyone should be valued and treated with respect.

Glad that things were going smoothly, Eric scanned their progress. The land had been cleared before they arrived, and the excavating had been done for the lower level. The masons were busy laying the block, with a goal to be done and ready for the first inspection by the end of the week, which meant they could start framing the following week. It was still spring, though, and Eric knew what that meant—there was always a potential for rain. Because of that, Eric was anxious to get the house framed and roofed on time. Once it was roofed, the trades could work inside, even in inclement weather.

The first week went by quickly. Even though the days were long, they went by fast, which is often the case when you're busy doing something you love. It helped that everyone got along and worked well together.

On Monday morning, however, they encountered their first problem. One of the carpenters showed up two hours late, which didn't sit well with Eric. The clock was ticking, and they were on a tight schedule to get the house framed and roofed. He needed his carpenters to be there and on time. This particular carpenter had a reputation for being late, but he also had a reputation for being quite skilled. He prided himself on doing things right the first time, every time. Concerned that this would become a pattern, Eric pulled him aside for a private talk.

"Hey, Ron. I just wanted to talk to see if there's a problem. I noticed you were a couple hours late.

Is there something wrong? Something I can help with?"

"Ah, no. It's no big deal. I just got a late start this morning. Don't worry, it won't set you back," he replied.

"I do want to make sure we stay on schedule—you know how important that is. But I also want to make sure that nobody is treated differently than anyone else. The rest of the crew was here before 7:00, ready to go, and they've been working ever since. It's not fair to expect them to be here on time if I don't expect it of everyone. Do you know what I mean?"

"What? If I put in a short day, what's it to you?"

"No. I'm just saying I want to see you make the same effort everyone else makes. We're a team, but I can't have people coming and going whenever they feel like it. I'm only trying to be fair. Can you work with me here?"

"Sure, whatever," Ron replied, although somewhat begrudgingly. "Now if you'll excuse me, I have to get back to work."

Eric didn't like confrontations, and he sensed that Ron didn't like what he'd had to say. He noticed that Ron didn't speak to him again for the rest of the day. Actually, he didn't speak much to anyone. Eric almost regretted saying anything to him at all, thinking that if he had just let it slide, it would have blown over and been an isolated incident.

Eric was relieved to see that Ron showed up on time for the rest of the week. Every day, Eric took the time to speak to him and let him know that he was happy with the work he was doing. While Ron's responses weren't super friendly, they were polite, leaving Eric to believe that they had put their earlier confrontation behind them, where it belonged.

On Friday afternoon, Eric ran into town to grab the checks to pay his subcontractors for their work, so they could pay their employees. He'd always believed in the motto that paid employees were happy employees. Having been in a position where money was short, Eric knew that paying people on time was not only expected, but also appreciated.

It was about an hour before quitting time when he noticed Ron was gone. The rest of the crew had just started wrapping up and were picking up their tools and cleaning the construction site, but Ron was nowhere to be found.

"Hey, guys, anyone seen Ron?" he yelled.

"Not recently," one replied.

"He took off about half an hour ago—said he had plans and had to leave early," another answered.

"What?" Eric couldn't believe what he'd just heard. But he knew he had to do something about it, even if it might offend the carpenter. The problem was he didn't know how to address the issue without creating a bigger rift.

He was still thinking about it on Sunday afternoon, so he decided to call Carl.

"Hi, Carl. I've been pretty busy this week, but I wanted to make sure I didn't forget to thank you for the tokens."

"My pleasure," Carl said. "So, do you have any insight on the new one, *Relationships*?"

"Well, I actually thought relationships were my forte and that was one token I didn't need. But it seems that I might be wrong," Eric admitted.

"How so? If I might ask, what's going on?"

Eric brought Carl up to date with what had happened during the week and Ron's response.

"You know, I thought I'd taken care of the problem, but it looks like that was only temporary."

"Eric, I won't tell you what to do. But I will tell you that there are relationships that should be cultivated and nurtured. Relationships that are based on trust are most valued and valuable. Let me ask you this: After one week working with this individual, do you trust him?"

Eric paused before answering. "I did, but now, I'm not so sure."

"Remember, too, Eric, that relationships aren't one-sided. That's why the best relationships are mutual and both parties benefit. That's why a relationship with a partner is so significant. Knowing that, can you say that your relationship with Ron is mutual and both of you benefit equally?"

"No, I can't. And that's the tough part—I gave him a chance and he let me down. Now I don't know how to handle it."

"Life is about relationships. The same is true for business. It is the relationships you create and bring with you that add value to the lives and businesses for all parties. That was the driving force behind our mastermind group, Eric. Every member was chosen quite carefully, not only for what they could gain, but also for what they could bring to the other members. Conduct your business in the same way, and you won't have any regrets. And remember, there are some relationships that are not beneficial. That is up to you to determine."

"Well, thank you, sir. I guess I have a lot to think about before tomorrow morning," Eric replied.

"Eric, don't make the mistake of making this personal. Any decision you make will affect everyone on the job site. It is a professional decision. Maybe that will help," Carl offered.

After the two hung up, Eric pondered the avenues he could take. He could pull Ron aside again and this time give him a sterner talk, making his expectations very clear. But Eric thought he'd already done that. And he thought he had treated Ronnie with respect. Unfortunately, though, that respect didn't appear to be mutual. If Ron had respected him as the general contractor and the leader of the project, he would have thanked him, apologized, and tried to do better. At the very least, Eric would have expected him to come to him if he had to leave early.

Hours later, Eric resigned himself to what he knew he had to do. His relationships with all of his subcontractors and trades were important to him. If he wanted their respect, he had to value their time, dedication, and commitment. They, too, deserved to have dependable workers to help them accomplish their jobs.

He picked up the phone and called Ron. After thanking him for the work he'd done, he advised him that his services weren't needed anymore.

The next morning, he advised his crew that Ron would not be returning. Then he took a few moments to thank them, letting them know that he appreciated their cooperation and dedication to the project and that he valued them. He assured them that he was reasonable and reminded them that he was there if they needed anything—his job was to make their jobs easier. One by one, they all shook his hand and thanked him.

"You can count on me, Eric. We've got a good group here. Let's get to work!" one said.

Eric smiled as he reached his hand into his pocket, finding the token, *Relationships*. Carl was right. Some relationships were worth tending to and nurturing. But sometimes relationships weren't mutually beneficial. He felt badly about letting Ron go, but he realized that he owed it to the people he could count on. It was his job to make sure they knew they could count on him.

Satisfied that his mission was accomplished, he made a mental note to let Carl know that he'd learned a valuable lesson. It was far better to invest in relationships based on trust and respect than to continually try to mend a one-sided relationship.

Chapter 8

Learn and Grow

There were a few more problems during the process, but nothing major. Work stalled for a couple days when the delivery of the kitchen cabinets was delayed. The tile installers had a scheduling conflict and Eric had to find someone else to install the bathroom tile and kitchen backsplash. (A damaged kitchen countertop had to be reordered, too.) But these were all things that Eric had taken into account when estimating the completion date. The building of a house took a coordinated effort, and it wasn't unusual for there to be an occasional or even unavoidable delay.

For the most part, Eric took it in stride. Whenever there was any issue, no matter how small, he communicated with his clients and kept them informed. He then recalculated the completion date and did whatever he could to make sure they stayed one step ahead of the game, if possible.

And it paid off—the house was built on schedule and within budget. The homeowners were more than satisfied with the end result. In the final walkthrough, they commented frequently on the attention to even the most minor detail and admired the quality and craftsmanship. It was precisely what they wanted and everything they had hoped this, their last home, would be. Not only did they say they were happy with the finished product, but they thanked Eric for making the process as painless as possible. He had kept them up to date with the status along the way and had consulted with them often when changes were necessary or decisions needed to be made.

Shortly before the house was completed, Eric received a card from Carl that included another token, *Learn and Grow*. This one was easy for Eric—it had been a learning process, and he had encountered obstacles while building the house but felt he had handled them well. And he was quick to share this with the older gentleman.

"It was a learning process, for sure. I also learned a lot about handling challenges and setbacks. Every time we were able to overcome them, work through the problem, and find a way to stay on track," he replied in an email.

"Very good then, but remember, too, that challenges can come in different shapes and sizes. They can be anticipated, or they can be unexpected and come out of nowhere. Unfortunately, Eric, obstacles don't just present themselves when you're in the learning stage—they happen to veteran business owners, too. It doesn't matter how much experience or money you have—it seems obstacles are nondiscriminatory. It's not the size of the obstacle that matters, but how you respond to it. It's all part of a hands-on education that cannot be taught in business or trade school. Having the desire and ability to admit that you need to learn more will one day be the measure of your success, mark my words," Carl wrote.

Their communications were less frequent after that. Carl indicated that he and his wife had plans to travel and enjoy their free time, but he promised to stay in touch. And from time to time, he did. Sometimes, he included a new token; most of the time, he did not. Eric received a postcard from Alaska and another from Paris, both wishing him well. Someday, Eric thought, he'd be in a position to enjoy the fruits of his labor, too.

The tokens he did receive came with no explanation, sometimes not even a note.

One was engraved with the words *Be Creative*. Another simply said *Initiative*. Eric understood both of those principles and didn't think they required a significant amount of contemplation, so he tossed them in the box where he kept all the wooden tokens he'd received from Carl.

There were two tokens, however, that weren't quite clear to Eric. The first he received in an envelope with a short note that said, "This one may be more important today than in the past. If you ignore it, it can erase everything you've created." Taking it out of the envelope, Eric turned the token over to find the words, *Tolerance and Understanding*. The other token came a month later and said *Profit by Failure*.

Well, I hope I never need that one, Eric thought.

Thus far, he hadn't. Business had been steady since he built that first home. He hadn't had to put feelers out, letting people know he was looking for work. As a matter of fact, work had been so steady that he'd had to turn away a couple of smaller jobs. A real estate developer had even been in contact with him about building a row of townhouses—a project Eric was more than enthusiastic about.

To Eric's delight and surprise, he was awarded the general contractor position on the townhouses. It was a major boost for him, one that would take his business to a whole new level. But it came with obstacles. For one thing, multifamily housing had different requirements and building codes that he had to learn and constantly refer to. In addition, the real estate developer who owned the land seemed to be meeting constantly with city officials about easements, ingress and egress requirements, underground utilities, and a variety of other building issues that related to developing virgin property.

Eric had a full-time crew and regular subcontractors to provide expertise in every aspect of the process. He had enough help that he was able to serve as general contractor without having to sling a hammer. This was new for him, but so was the learning curve as he got a firsthand education about property development.

Max, the developer, had a generous amount of patience. He knew that Eric didn't have any experience with the intricacies of property development or multifamily housing, but he was willing to take the time to teach him. Having a capable general contractor who was willing to learn how to do things the right way and according to regulations was beneficial to him. Besides, he really liked Eric and admired his work ethic and commitment. He was happy to teach Eric what he didn't know, but there were certain qualities that couldn't be taught. You either had them or you didn't He was glad Eric had them.

Eric had forgotten what it was like to start from scratch, having to learn something new each and every day. Sometimes it was mind boggling, but at the same time, it was energizing. It was rewarding to know that he was expanding not only his knowledge, but also his experience and abilities.

The steady work came with a downside, however. Eric found that he just didn't have the time to complete his cabin renovation. Every night when he walked in the door he promised himself that he'd get back to the renovations over the weekend, but he often found himself on the job site when Saturday morning rolled around. Reminding himself that the cabin could wait, he put it on the backburner. He knew his priorities.

After they broke ground on the fourth townhouse, Max asked him to accompany him to look at another parcel of land. This one was quite different from the wide open plain they'd been building on. Also undeveloped, it consisted of acres of wooded land.

"This land would require a totally different style of development, Eric," Max advised. "Rows of modern townhouses or apartment buildings would be out of place here. Besides, it's too far out from the main hub of the city to appeal to apartment dwellers. Take a look around and let me know your thoughts."

Looking around at the undisturbed land, Eric's thoughts immediately went to his cabin. Suddenly, he could see rural single-family housing, large one-acre lots with established trees, big porches, and ample windows from which to admire the view. One area specifically looked like the perfect central location to house a neighborhood park.

"Max, when I look at this land, I see upscale family housing. Imagine something with more of a country feel, maybe even slightly rustic. Something like large log cabins with great rooms, lofts, and big porches. Don't misunderstand—I'm thinking of impressive residences, not primitive log cabins. The natural beauty of the cabins would fit well into the scenery and be enhanced by the beauty and shade of these beautiful trees," he said.

"Yes! I can see it—large log cabin homes for the suburban upper middle-class family that wants to get away from the hustle and bustle. I can even see a couple of kids and a dog on those front porches," Max said excitedly.

"You know, I knew this land appealed to me, but I couldn't picture what to do with it. It's out of my expertise, but I'm willing to try something new. So what do you say—are you ready to take the next step? Want to become a partner with me on this development and take it under your wing? I would make the financial investment, while you undertook the design and development. Sound good?"

Max was smiling, anticipating Eric's response, but Eric was struggling not to show his initial terror at being responsible for something so big. All of his old fears came to the surface, and he was bombarded with "What-ifs." What if he screwed this up? What if he wasn't ready to assume so much responsibility?

Still, he knew it was a once-in-a-lifetime opportunity, and he'd be crazy to pass it up. Then he reminded himself that it was precisely what he'd always wanted—to be a prominent builder who was involved in major developments. He just hadn't been prepared for it to really happen. But here it was … and Max was still waiting for an answer.

"Are you sure, Max? That's a lot of responsibility; maybe you want someone more experienced," Eric replied.

"I don't make decisions or offers on a whim, Eric. I respect your initiative and your desire to learn. Those are admirable qualities. I have the utmost faith in you—I knew I wanted you to see this land because it was out of my 'norm.' I thought it was an opportunity for us to work together in some capacity at a different level. It wasn't until we got here that I knew what that would entail. I know that doing something new can be uncomfortable sometimes, but this type of development would be new to both of us. We can learn together."

"Well, then, I'm in. You've made me an offer I can't refuse, and I want you to know I appreciate it. I hope I don't let you down," Eric said.

"You won't, partner. I believe in you. You're ready," Max smiled and shook Eric's hand.

It was a deal … and Eric immediately remembered who he really had to thank: Carl. Carl had taken him under his wing and offered him the advice that came from experience. Carl, who had been his grandfather's friend, Carl who had believed in him and opened up a vault of wisdom from an elite group of multimillionaires.

He knew he wouldn't be where he was today if it weren't for the kindness and generosity of his friend, Carl. That night, he sat down at the computer and wrote him an appreciative email.

My friend, Carl,

I wanted to send you my deepest appreciation for the wisdom you've so unselfishly shared with me. Because of you, and your tokens, I have grown and so has my business. Today I was offered an opportunity to partner with a real estate developer in the creation and building of large upscale log cabin homes. I accepted the offer, knowing that I do have a lot to learn. But as you've shown me, one cannot grow unless one is continually learning. Know that as you are traveling around the world, I am stepping into a new world as well—hopefully, one that brings prosperity and even more growth.

And it would never have been possible without you.
Eric

Chapter 9

Overcoming Obstacles

Purchasing and surveying the property had been a long process, and it was months before Eric would receive the go-ahead to begin excavation. Before any lots could be sold or construction could begin, they first had to install drainage pipes, water supply lines, and other critical utility services on the land.

Finally, it was time. When Eric arrived, the bulldozers were lined up and ready to begin. The game plan was to excavate as sparingly as possible and remove only those trees that were absolutely necessary.

Homeowners would then determine which trees they wanted to keep and which trees to remove before construction of their custom homes.

Eric couldn't help but feel excited, although, admittedly, he was nervous at the same time. He knew the success of this development would either make or break him. He wished Max was there for reassurance that everything would go smoothly, but his friend and partner had business out of state and had left everything up to Eric. "You'll be fine. You've got the checklist and timeline of everything that needs to be done. And don't forget, we're working with professionals. The surveyors and excavators know what they're doing. Just don't forget to wear your hard hat! Safety first!" he laughed.

Standing on the sidelines, Eric watched as the operators climbed onto the bulldozers and revved up their engines. On schedule, they broke ground just after 8:00 a.m. Like Max said, these guys were professionals. They knew what they were doing and had planned and coordinated the process. Starting at the east end of the development, they would work south and then progress to the west, a less wooded area where the plans were to build a community park and small nature trail.

They made steady progress, scooping out buckets of dirt and strategically placing them in mounds to the side. What was once undisturbed land was now taking on the appearance of a construction in progress. Eric was somewhat mesmerized by it as he watched the ground being turned and the brush and small trees effortlessly being removed from the landscape.

With day one completed and in the books, Eric watched as the equipment was properly secured for the night. The fuel truck would arrive early in the morning to refuel the equipment, making sure the crew could get back to work without delays or down time. For now, there was nothing to do but call it a day and a successful one at that.

* * *

The next morning was a repeat of the day before. Everyone knew what they were supposed to do and didn't have to wait for instructions. Eric's role was to observe and communicate with the supervisors on site, who kept him informed about their progress and what they expected to be able to complete by the end of the day.

It was midmorning when he was approached by Jake, who worked for the excavation company.

"Hey, Eric, there are some gentlemen here who want to talk to you," he said.

"Okay," he said, jumping on the four-wheeler to follow Jake.

When they arrived, the bulldozer had been shut down and the operator was standing to the side talking with two men.

"What's going on?" Eric asked.

Jake walked him over and introduced Eric as the developer.

"We just wanted to check out what's going on here. I understand that you're going to build new homes on this land. But did you know that this spot right here where we're standing is a historic battlefield? In fact, the previous owner granted us permission to have reenactments here every year," one of the men said.

"A historic battlefield? Really?" Eric asked. "Well, I'm not sure what to do about that. We purchased the land, and it was never disclosed to us. It's not protected land or a landmark or anything, is it?"

"Not officially. But if we need to, we can begin the process. Our main concern is paying respect to the lives lost here and what they fought for."

"You mean you're really going to try to stop us from building houses on our own land?" Eric asked.

"We thought we'd first approach you and see if we could work this out on friendly terms. A historic battleground is a big deal, and if you break ground on this section, you're going to upset a lot of people," the second man replied.

"What people?"

"Veterans, for one. That includes members of the American Legion, Veterans of Foreign Wars, and even Daughters of the American Revolution. Then there are the families whose ancestors fought for freedom and liberty. Battlefields represent something significant to them, especially those fought on our soil. What happened on this land affected their lineage and, quite honestly, our country."

Eric contemplated what they said, realizing that he did, indeed, have an issue and one that could greatly impact the public's perception of their development.

The operator spoke first.

"What do you want us to do, boss?"

"I'm going to have to make some phone calls. Maybe the crew should break early for lunch until I have some answers," Eric said. Then, turning to the two men, he said, "Can you stick around for a few minutes and show me just where the boundaries are for this battlefield and how big it is?"

"Sure. We can give you a general idea, if that helps."

"Good. As soon as I know what we're working with, Jake, we can get the crew working outside of the area," informed Eric. "In the meantime, why don't you move the dozers over to the west end, away from this particular area," Eric suggested. Within 30 minutes the job site was silent. The machines were shut down, and all of the excavators had taken off in their company trucks, leaving Eric standing with the two men.

"Okay, so how about we walk the property and you two can show me just where this battlefield is?" asked Eric.

As they walked, the men gave Eric some background. According to them, the location for the battle had been specifically chosen because of its hills, which provided cover. In addition, the location marked the boundary between two territories and was heavily defended to prevent the opposition from advancing into occupied territory.

"Who won?" Eric asked, suddenly curious. History had always interested him and here he was standing on the very ground where history was made—history that might have actually changed our country.

"It doesn't matter, does it?" one man replied. "Both sides lost men and even more were injured. What we focus on is that sacrifice—that willingness to go into battle for our country. None of those men are still with us today, but we can honor them all by protecting the site where they fought for us."

"You've got a point," Eric admitted.

When they were done, Eric estimated that the battlefield encompassed approximately 20 acres of their land, as well as additional land outside the property's boundaries, which was undeveloped as well. His mind automatically began calculating the cost of the lots and the potential loss if they couldn't sell them. The numbers were significant enough that he knew he needed to call Max.

"Thank you for sharing this information with me," Eric said. "I'm going to have to talk with my partner and explore our options. In the meantime, I assure you that we won't touch this area, at least not until we have some answers and have tried to reach some agreement with you. If you could leave me with your phone numbers, I will give you a call in the next couple of days."

After exchanging their contact information, the men left the site, confident that Eric would keep his word. And he fully intended to, but he needed advice. Taking his phone out of his pocket, he sent Max a text, hoping to catch him at a good time.

Hey, ran into a snag here. Need advice. Call as soon as you can.

Ten minutes later, Max did just that.

"What's up, Eric?"

"Well, we just had a couple visitors on the job site here. They're saying this property contains part of a historic battlefield, and they're willing to do what it takes to protect it. This is foreign territory for me. What should I do?"

"A battlefield? Now, that's interesting. Who would have guessed? How much land are they talking about?" Max asked.

"Roughly 20 acres on the east end where the property butts up to the undeveloped property to the north."

"You know, we weren't developing all of that land anyway. Isn't part of that area supposed to remain scenic, providing a wide open view to the north?"

"Yes, some, but I'm guessing we'll lose about 20 lots or so," Eric answered.

"Well, Eric, we can't just go on their word. We have to have some sort of documentation or proof before we do anything," advised Max.

"How do I get that?" Eric asked.

"I'd start with an online search for the local historical society. Maybe look at newspaper archives for articles about the battlefield and the annual reenactments. That should give you something to start with."

"And, Eric, play nice. Make sure you let these guys know that we are respectful of their position and want to work with them to come to a mutually acceptable solution. We don't want to ruffle any feathers, especially at the beginning stages before the lots go on the market. If this is a historic battlefield and the word gets out that we're not willing to work with them, they can make us look bad to the public, and we don't want that. The saying, 'Any publicity is good publicity' does not apply in this business."

"Okay, I'll get on it right away," Eric said.

"Good. I've got a meeting in a few minutes. Let me know how it goes."

Great, looks like I'm on my own. Well, time's a-wastin',
he thought. *I'd better call Jake and give them the rest of the
day off. They can start on the west end tomorrow.*

Eric picked up the phone again.

"Yeah, that's what I expected. Don't worry, though,
Eric. We'll be back to work in the morning. I'm sure
you'll get this sorted out in day or two," Jake said.

"I hope so, but I think it's going to take a bit longer.
We need to verify the claims and then establish the
boundaries. Then we're going to have to figure out
a solution, and who knows how long that's going to
take?" Eric replied. "You never know with these things.
All we can do is wait."

With a big sigh, Eric resigned himself to the situation at hand. It was his first development and here he
was with his hands tied, unable to work.

Eric spent the rest of the day at the library, where
he researched newspaper archives about reenactments
and the history of the area. The men were right—the
Gazette had reported an annual event for the last ten
years. From there, he tracked down the county's historical society by phone, where a friendly woman directed
him to old black-and-white photographs of soldiers and
other memorabilia in the library archives, confirmed
that there was, indeed, a battle fought on the hilly ter-
rain that was one of the more appealing characteristic of
the land. Although Eric knew he had all the information he needed, he remained there for two more hours,
finding the documentation and history of the land and
surrounding area to be fascinating.

After receiving photocopies of several documents,
Eric returned to his own little cabin, thinking that now

was a good time to tackle a few small projects he'd been putting off. His mind couldn't switch itself off from the situation, however, and he spent the evening sitting by the river, contemplating different scenarios. He knew that if they attempted to sell a single lot that sat on the battlefield, it would impact people's desire to live there. The press would have a field day with it, and the entire development would suffer as a result. No matter how this played out, it probably wasn't going to be good.

Needing to spend some of his nervous energy, he took a walk down the lane, eventually finding himself at Carl's cabin, which looked precisely the same as it had the last time he'd been there, months before. Sitting at the old kitchen table where he'd first talked to the stranger who quickly became both a mentor and a friend, he wondered what Carl would do in this situation.

I guess there's one way to find out, he thought and picked up his phone to send Carl an email.

Explaining the events of the day, Eric vented his frustration and asked Carl for advice. Within an hour, he received a reply.

Ah, an obstacle and a big one at that. I knew it would eventually happen. Growth always brings a new set of challenges. I admit that this one, though, is unusual. My advice to you is to cooperate and do what's right. You have to recognize when you cannot control a situation and can only control your response to it. Now that you know what you're dealing with, you can adjust your plans and act accordingly. I know this might seem like a major setback right now, but don't overlook the fact that in every obstacle you will face, there is an opportunity. Find that opportunity. It's there, I assure you. You might have to do some digging and soul searching, but I have faith that you can find a way to overcome this with minimal damage. Keep me posted.

Your friend,

Carl

Eric read the email and then read it again, each time looking for that single nugget of advice that would help him do the right thing, whatever that was. But it wasn't there—the email was too vague, and while his words offered much-needed support and reassurance, they lacked the advice he really wanted. With no other options, he accepted the fact that, for now, he could only hope that the answers would come to him soon.

First, he called one of the gentlemen who had visited the site and brought him up to date.

"I just wanted to let you know that we're working on a solution—hopefully, one that works for both of us. But if there is no objection, we would like to continue clearing the land on the west end. I assure you, we will create a large buffer around the area and avoid it until we have a plan."

The man readily agreed and even thanked Eric. "I really appreciate your willingness to work with us here. We wouldn't have stepped in if it wasn't so important, not only to us, but to the community at large. The historic aspect of the property deserves to be preserved, in our opinion."

"After doing my own research, I tend to agree with you. If you can give me a couple of days to talk with my partner and review our options, I'd appreciate it," Eric replied.

After hanging up the phone, Eric remembered Carl's advice. It wasn't the problem itself that would impact the success or failure of the development, but rather how they responded to the problem.

It was time to sit down and look at their options. Then, and only then, would he feel like he could respond appropriately.

Chapter 10

Tolerance and Understanding

Before making any decisions, Eric was curious to learn how other historic battlefields had been treated or preserved. Maybe they could simply erect a monument marking the site and that would be sufficient. But in his heart, he knew it wasn't. A quick Google search led him to historical sites from the War of 1812, the French and Indian War, and the Civil War. Actually, he was surprised by the number of battles that had taken place across the United States. On the east coast, there was the Battle of Bunker Hill, the Battle of Saratoga, the Battle of Princeton, and the Battle of Long Island. Mississippi was home to the Vicksburg Campaign, and Chalmette was the site of the Battle of New Orleans. Both the Alamo and the Battle of San Jacinto occurred in Texas. Among the most tragic were the Battle of the Little Bighorn, which took place in Montana, and the Wounded Knee Massacre in South Dakota. And these were only the tip of the iceberg—those that were considered some of the most important in U.S. history.

Notebook in hand, he wrote down every name and the dates that corresponded with them. Then he dug further to learn about who now owned the land and how it was being used. The largest and most historic battlegrounds had become national parks and were owned and protected by the federal government. Insofar as documented smaller sites were concerned, it was clear that most of those had also been preserved in some way, rather than becoming parking lots, shopping malls, or even housing developments. It was becoming readily evident to Eric what they had to do. Whether they rightfully owned the land or not was a moot issue. The eastern section of the property was not theirs to develop. It belonged to those who had fought and sacrificed. It represented freedom and liberty and needed to be recognized as such.

It was time to call Max.

"Max, I've been researching the history of our country's battlegrounds, and I have to tell you it's been quite a learning experience. First, you need to know that the larger sites have become national parks. Even the smaller ones that I found are left untouched and undeveloped."

"Okay, so what do you propose we do? Remember, we do own the property," Max reminded him.

"I admit I'm not well versed on the mechanics of these things and how to officially proceed, but if we're going to do the right thing—and I don't think we have a choice—we cannot build on that land. It simply has too much historic significance. Besides, it would imply a lack of respect and compassion for the military, veterans, and their descendants, not to mention patriotism. I'm unfamiliar with how to do it, but this isn't our land anymore. It belongs in the hands of those who will preserve its rich history and will pay homage to it."

"Are you saying we should sell it? To who?" Max asked.

"No, not sell it. You see, it was never ours to buy. That land belongs to history, not whoever legally holds the deed. We need to separate the parcel and deed it back to the government."

"That's our only option, huh?" Max asked. "That's not what I wanted to hear, but I guess you're right. Now that we know what we're dealing with, we can't ignore it."

"No, we can't. We have to take into consideration what happened here and respect the feelings of those who serve our country and their families. This might be a setback for us, but it's something far bigger for them," Eric agreed.

"Both my dad and grandfather were enlisted men, Eric," Max said softly. "Figure out what we have to do to make this right and let me know. I'll contact my legal staff and make sure they're on board and ready to expedite matters."

Eric made some phone calls, inviting key people to a meeting, hoping they would know how to proceed. Before any official moves were made, he wanted to hear their thoughts and ideas. Maybe they knew of other options or were entertaining different ideas. When he walked into the meeting later that week, he recognized the two gentlemen who had visited the job site, who had brought with them a couple of others from their organization. Also attending were several county officials, including a representative from the recorder of deed's office, a county historian, the president of the park board, and even the mayor. They had all agreed that there was some urgency to the issue and were willing to change their schedules to accommodate the meeting.

After introductions were made, Eric thanked everyone for attending and brought them up to date on what had transpired.

"First, I'd like to thank you for coming today. I hope I can provide you with some insight and information that will assist us in moving forward. As you know, we are in the beginning stages of creating a new housing development, but it has been brought to our attention that a segment of the property is the site of a historic battle that occurred right here in our community. I'm sure most of you are familiar with the battle and the area," Eric said.

"Before I continue, I do want to let you all know we had no knowledge of this, nor was it ever disclosed to us before we purchased the land, which I understand includes about 20 acres of this battlefield. If we had known, we probably would not be sitting here today," advised Eric. "But now that we do know that the property includes a historic site, we want to work with the community and the government to rectify the situation."

Eric then opened the floor, asking the attendees to share their thoughts and opinions. The unanimous consensus was that the battlefield was a historic site, even without official recognition, and it should be treated as such. Several people added that they understood this was a unique situation and offered their understanding to Eric and Max, noting the hardship it placed on them.

Eric advised that although no final decisions had yet been made, they were roping off the area and creating a buffer zone. Any work on the east end of the property had been temporarily halted. He then requested assistance in determining the official boundaries of the battlefield. From there, they discussed a few other options, including rezoning the land, which was currently zoned as residential. They also asked the historian if she could provide the group with information about the necessary steps, should they opt to declare the land a historic landmark.

"What happens from here will depend on us and everyone else who is involved," Eric said. "I wanted to bring this matter to your attention and seek your counsel and opinions before we make any final decisions."

After the meeting, members of the American Legion approach Eric.

"You know, we came here ready to be on the defensive and fight to preserve history and respect the lives that were sacrificed on your land. But we didn't need to. We don't often meet with developers who are so understanding and willing not only to hear us out, but also to actually accommodate our wishes. Thank you."

Those words humbled Eric. "It's become apparent that what we have here is larger, much larger, than a housing development. I respect that, and I respect you and those who have sacrificed for our right to purchase land and build what we want. But that doesn't mean that building what we want is the right thing to do. We will build, I assure you. However, we will have to make some changes and probably some sacrifices. Compared to the sacrifices you gentlemen have made, though, they're minimal. So don't thank me. Thank *you*," Eric replied.

When he called Max later, his friend was happy to hear that the meeting was amicable. "I'm glad you brought everyone to the table at the beginning," he said. "With their agreement and cooperation, we might be able to resolve this faster than we think," Max said. "Now that you have put the wheels into motion, I think it's time for us to move on and figure out how we're going to adjust our plans for the site."

* * *

When he returned home, Eric listed his options. First, he could try to apply reason and somehow persuade everyone concerned to allow them to build on the battlefield. It was an option, but not a realistic one. Second, they could build and still pay homage by erecting a monument on the land that conveyed its historic significance. Third, they could maintain ownership of the land but have it rezoned to prevent any development by them or any future owners of the property. Fourth, they could deed the entire parcel to an appropriate organization and turn the control of the land over to them.

Wondering what Carl might suggest, he emailed them.

Carl's reply wasn't what he'd expected, however.

Eric,

You have listed four options here, and each is feasible, although perhaps not all will be well received. Each is also obvious. When it comes to major obstacles such as these, it would be wise to move beyond the obvious. Get creative. Somewhere in this dilemma lies a solution that not only conveys your acceptance, but also your understanding and compassion. Remember, what has happened is not your fault, but it is not the fault of the veterans and their descendants and preservation groups either. They want the same thing you want—preservation of the battlefield in a way that shows both respect and appreciation. Put your thinking cap on—there doesn't have to be a winner and a loser. With the right solution, everyone will feel like they benefitted and be confident that the right thing was done for all concerned.

You've got this,

Carl

Another solution? Carl wanted him to come up with another solution, but try as he might, Eric couldn't see one. It was either black or white—the area belonged to the developers or it belonged to some other person or organization who could stake a claim to it. Not only had Carl encouraged him to find a win-win, but he'd also told him to be compassionate and understanding.

Hmm, the tokens again. They seem to keep coming up again, even after he'd forgotten about them.

That night Eric pulled out the box of tokens, thinking that one of them might lead him toward a solution. One by one, he flipped them over, rubbing his thumb across their smooth, worn wood surfaces. He wondered just how many other hands had held these tokens and how many others had found the answers they were looking for by the words engraved on them. Maybe his grandfather had touched each and every one, he thought. Oh, how he wished his grandfather was there to help him with this predicament.

The closest thing he had was Carl, and while Carl had been a strong influence, he had left the ultimate decision to Eric. But not before subtly letting him know that the choices he'd presented hadn't won his whole-hearted approval.

Knowing that, he pulled out the blueprints. Maybe there was something there that he'd overlooked. Maybe, just maybe, if he looked at them long enough, the answer would come to him—a solution that showed understanding and compassion—one that revealed a tolerance of others and their experiences and passions, both in the past and in the present.

Examining the plans, he wished he knew just how large the battlefield site was—that would impact any plan he made. However, the expert had estimated that it was about twenty acres. Taking into account the buffer zone that they'd established, he blocked off a rough section and then contemplated the remaining development possibilities. He tossed around options, but failed to come up with anything other than variations of the options he'd posed to Carl.

A couple of cups of coffee and an hour later, he'd almost ditched the effort, thinking it was just his luck that his first project as a developer would come with such large-scale problems. Of all the properties they could have chosen, they just had to choose this one. Shaking his head, he realized that the reasons they'd chosen the land might coincide with why it was chosen as a site for battle. It offered high, dry land that provided cover and shelter, as well as hills and boroughs. There was an open park-like setting as well, but—unfortunately for Eric and Max—the site could not be a park. It was Eric's belief that nothing should disturb the tranquility of a site that was home to fallen American soldiers.

Then it hit him. He had a solution and one that could not only work for Eric and Max, but also paid tribute to the battlefield and military and veteran wishes. While it would require some replotting and new blueprints, it was feasible. Underground utilities and water supply and drainage lines hadn't yet been installed, so that wasn't a consideration. In the end, Eric smiled. It could even be a selling point for their development. Grabbing a pen, he wrote the words "Liberty Trails" on a piece of paper and began to document his idea.

Chapter 11

Profit by Failure

Eric awoke early and waited impatiently until it was a respectable time to call Max. Both excited and nervous, he couldn't wait to pass his idea onto him and hear his partner's opinion. At 8 a.m. sharp, he made the call.

"Max, do you have a minute? I think I just might have a solution to our historic battlefield problem, and I'd love to hear your opinion," he said.

"Well, you sound excited. Sure, I've got a few minutes. Go ahead."

"Okay. Keep in mind that we want to respect our service members and veterans and their sacrifices. According to everything I've heard, the best way to do that is to make sure the land remains undeveloped and the site is undisturbed. We already know what that means—we cannot develop that property," Eric explained.

"All right. I get that," Max replied.

"Now, we also know that neither of us wants to abandon the project. It will be a huge financial loss for you and a major career setback for me. There is the possibility that we could create a buffer zone and build around the site. We'd have to take our losses and figure out how much profit margin we have left. By reducing the size of the lots, we could make up some of that loss, but I think that would be less appealing to potential buyers," Eric continued.

"I can see you've thought this out, so what do you propose?" Max asked.

"I say let's make this battlefield a focal point and build the development around it. We'd erect a fence and create a buffer zone to protect and preserve the area, and then build a walking trail that goes around it and through the entire development. On the outer boundary, we'd lose several lots, but we could erect a community building there. I'll get back to that in a second. Max, we'd keep the log cabin theme, but join it with the historic aspect of battlefields. Strategically placed along the walking trail would be signs that provide education and information about the battles fought here and in surrounding areas. Oh, and we'd name the development 'Liberty Trails' and erect a monument at the entrance."

"Interesting. Unique. You know, Eric, I'd have to see the plans and, of course, we'd have to get approval from the appropriate authorities, but it might just work," Max agreed.

"There's more—I was thinking that the community building could be used for meetings, parties, and events for veterans. We could rent it out to individuals or organizations. Inside, it would pay tribute to the history of the land and what the soldiers fought for. We could even offer the oversight and management of the community building to veterans—there are plenty out there, and they're very dedicated to those who have fought before and alongside them. There are plenty of groups, like the American Legion, Veterans of Foreign Wars, the Daughters of the American Revolution. Even the National Guard hosts community events and memorials. Can you see it? Can you see how we can turn this major obstacle into a selling point that actually benefits our development and appeals to both the public and the historic and military communities?"

"I think you're onto something, Eric. Do me a favor, will you, and give a call to our architects. Sit down with them and explain just what you proposed to me and see how quickly they can develop new plans," Max said.

"Sure thing! I'll call them as soon as we hang up. In the meantime, though, how do I handle our next meeting? I don't want to reveal too much, just in case it won't fly. But I do want them to know that we are diligently working on an alternative that will protect the battlefield and pay homage to veterans."

"I understand, Eric. You know, sometimes it is the way we handle things that determines the outcome.

The situation we are in is already a delicate one, and you have to be prepared to deal with different personalities, as well as the missions and desires of different organization. As you've probably learned, they have had to advocate and fight for the preservation of their history and beliefs in a society that doesn't always respect the sacrifices they've witnessed. It's a shame, but sometimes developers only see dollar signs, and come hell or high water, they're going to do what it takes to get their money, even if it creates hardship or infringes on someone's beliefs," he said. Letting out a chuckle, he continued. "That drive is probably okay when dealing with government bureaucrats and the red tape they can strangle us with, but not when it comes to the respected groups we're dealing with here. We want to be developers who are welcomed by communities, not developers who are feared or worse, ostracized at every turn."

"So what do I do?" Eric asked.

"See how quickly you can get plans created first. When you walk into the meeting, repeat that we respect their beliefs and want to work with them to find a mutually acceptable solution. Make it very clear that you agree that the battlefield site should remain intact and undisturbed and ask them to consider working with us to create a development that pays tribute to the injured and fallen soldiers and becomes a historic landmark for the entire community. Oh, that's another thing—contact the historical society and find out what we have to do to get the county to declare the site a historical landmark. That means that we'll have to give them some level of input in

the development and plans, but it is a good faith
move. I think you'll find that the different parties will
appreciate that you've already explored the idea—it
provides them with verification that we're not just
saying what they want to hear, but ready and willing
to act on it," Max offered.

"Got it," Eric said while quickly jotting down notes
on his tablet. "So, Max, do you really think this could
fly?"

"I think it's got potential, real potential. That
doesn't mean it's not going to be without problems.
There is a lot of work to be done and layers of approval
before we can get started again. And it hasn't escaped
my attention that we're going to lose some lot sales,
which will dip into our profits ... and we have no
idea how much the fence, the trail, the community
building, or the plaques and signs will cost. It could
be significant, but it's better than abandoning the
project—and I don't like the thought of rezoning or
splitting the land and selling it off. Who knows, Eric,
Liberty Trails might appeal to homeowners so much
that the lots sell themselves!"

Eric laughed. "I'm not so sure that's going to
happen. I would have been happy if the log cabins had
been the big appeal here."

"It looks like we'll never know. But there is one
thing I do know, Eric, and it's that I admire you for
having the vision and creativity to find a viable solution.
There are a lot of developers who would have stuck
adamantly to their original plans, fought to the end,
and probably lost the public's approval. There are also
some who would have cut their losses right away and

thrown in the towel, writing the project off as a failure," Max said.

"If it was only up to you, what would you have done, Max?"

"That's hard to say. I think I would have tried to salvage whatever we could of the project, but that's another thing we'll never know. You, on the other hand, found an angle that not only cuts our losses, but also leaves plenty of room for profit, if we play it right. I'm amazed and impressed. Just a couple days ago, I was beginning to believe that this purchase and development was a failure," he said.

After hanging up the phone, Eric made an appointment to meet with the architects that afternoon, figuring that once he was done there, he'd stop in at the historical society for a discussion. That done, he called Carl, anxious to share his plan with him.

"I'm impressed, young man," Carl said with sincerity.

"I couldn't have done it without you. And the tokens. I was at my wit's end and about ready to throw in the towel when I pulled out the tokens you'd given me. Then I started to wonder how my grandpa would have dealt with this situation, and how your mastermind group of multimillionaires would have reacted," Eric said.

"And what was your guess?" Carl asked.

"I figured that they had become successful because they didn't stop when they encountered obstacles. Actually, it might have inspired them even more. I have to admit that facing failure is challenging. Coming up with possible solutions is even more difficult. But, Carl,

I discovered that there's something really rewarding about knowing you can find a solution if you look hard enough—and that the solution can actually become a positive for everyone. It really makes you feel like you've moved a mountain and accomplished something."

"That's what sets apart leaders and those who are successful from those who are not, Eric. Successful people don't give up. If they want something, they find a way to make it happen. To them, obstacles are temporary setbacks. Some even believe they are opportunities. All of them know that there is no such thing as failure, even if they do have to abandon their plans. They know that the only failure is the inability to learn something valuable. Experience is a very valuable lesson, as I'm sure you now know."

"I can see that now. It sure makes my former problems seem small," Eric laughed. "I have to admit, I was feeling a little self-pity—I'd just been given a huge opportunity that had turned into a lemon."

"But you turned it from something that left a bitter taste in your mouth to something that could actually be very appealing to a lot of people. It takes persistence to do that, as well as passion and dedication. And sometimes you have to let go of your original ideas—it's like the 3M employee, what's his name? Ah, yes, Spencer Silver. Anyway, he created the adhesive for post-it notes, you know, those sticky notes people put on everything nowadays. Well, it was too light to adhere to anything and not permanent, so management deemed it unusable. Years later, a guy named Arthur Fry found a use for it and Post-It notes became a phenomenon, a household word. You see, Silver was creating an adhesive, but it wasn't quite the glue he was originally going for. It took Fry to see that it had other possibilities and that those possibilities were even bigger and better than the original idea."

Max continued. "You did the same thing, Eric. You were creating a development, but unforeseen circumstances threw a wrench in your plans. You didn't abandon your plan, though. You found a way to turn your development into something that did work, even though it wasn't how you originally envisioned it would be. It's the mark of success, Eric. Your grandfather was quite good at it, too. He was adept at figuring out a way to profit from failure. He'd be proud of you. I know I am," Carl stated.

"Thank you. That really means a lot to me. Now, I just have to sell this idea to the powers that be and hope everyone concerned can see this is a win-win for all of us. But first I have to meet with the architects and hope they can grasp the concept and portray it well on paper. Wish me luck!" Eric said.

"Luck has nothing to do with it, Eric. Take another look at those tokens and read what they say. The tokens will provide you with what you need," Carl assured him.

Chapter 12

Gratitude

Six months after discovering that they owned historic ground, construction of the first home began for Eric and Max. The first model built perfectly illustrated how the old could be combined with the new in an upscale log cabin home with all the modern conveniences. Once the tentative plans for the site had been released by the press, interest was piqued, and homeowners were drawn to the development. It certainly hadn't been the fast and easy path Eric would have liked to have taken, but he was satisfied with the outcome.

A ceremony was held to dedicate the community building and battlefield. Participating in the ceremony were representatives from veterans groups and the National Guard, all of whom had welcomed the opportunity to share their opinions and provide input on the development. Ultimately, it became a joint venture, but it wouldn't have been possible without Carl and his tokens.

As Carl had told him, luck would have nothing to do with the ultimate success or failure of the development for Eric. Instead, the tokens provided him with everything he needed. That remark enticed Eric to once again pull out and contemplate the tokens and the advice Carl had imparted. There was one token in particular which guided Eric in developing a solution that would respect and honor all parties: Illuminate.

Illuminate: shining light on a problem instead of sweeping it under a rug. If Eric's initial plan to build over the site had actually been realized, it most certainly would have been met with protest. Any attempt to ignore the issue would have caused even bigger problems, to the detriment of the whole project.

Realizing that the only way to resolve the situation was to acknowledge it and, as the developers, accept responsibility for arriving at an acceptable solution, Eric delivered his revised proposal with an air of excitement and compassion. He immediately let it be known that they understood the seriousness of the situation and would entertain any reasonable ideas or alternatives to his proposal. Being willing to cooperate gave all parties the means to work together to reach an amicable solution.

As a result, the problem had been transformed into the focal selling point of the development. Judging by the attendance at the ribbon cutting, the public loved the idea of a new home that was reminiscent of the past, while being part of a patriotic community.

Max opened the event by welcoming all, giving special recognition to military and veteran organizations. Keeping the dedication short and sweet, he provided an overview of the development and how it honored the history of the community and the nation. He was followed by the American Legion members who led the Pledge of Allegiance at the flagpole that marked the entrance to the community building, followed by the traditional playing of "Taps" to honor patriots and fallen soldiers alike.

Then he turned the mike over to Eric, who was not accustomed to being in the limelight and had not come prepared to make a speech.

"Thank you everyone for your support, especially those who have served or are serving our country and freedom. While I do not have a speech prepared, I want to express my gratitude to everyone who made this development possible. First, I'd like to thank my partner, Max, for giving me this opportunity. I'd also like to thank a good friend, Carl, and the other entrepreneurs who provided me with the support and guidance to make it happen. To all of the veterans and their organizations, government officials, and historians, your input and suggestions were crucial and appreciated. My building crew deserves recognition for their skill and craftsmanship in creating the model home you are all invited to tour. While you're there, take note of the furnishings and interior design courtesy of our very talented interior designer, Heather."

The ribbon was then cut, signifying the official opening, and the public was invited to tour the grounds where plaques honoring the historic battle had been strategically placed, followed by one official ring of the large bronze liberty bell that proudly stood on the lawn outside the community building.

Rather than joining in the outdoor activities, Eric walked to the model home. He had worked diligently with the architect to custom design this home, making sure it contained the detail he had always insisted on, while providing the amenities today's homeowners desired. In the end, even Eric was impressed with the three-bedroom, two-bath log home. From every perspective, it offered a different view and vantage point, whether sitting on the large wooden porch or looking down from the upstairs loft. It did not escape his attention, though, that the home wouldn't have been nearly as impressive without the assistance of the interior designer who had staged it so well. Heather had scoured antique shops to find just the right furnishings and accessories to make both new and old join together in a timeless and functional way.

It was everything he'd dreamed it would be, and the public seemed to agree. The months that followed brought with them the sale of many lots, and in less than a year, there was only one lot left. This was a corner lot that Eric had developed an affinity for because it was positioned against homes on one side and the walking trail on the other. The back of the property overlooked the battlefield, which was in the process of being declared a park to preserve its rich history.

Everything had worked out for the best, but Eric knew that it wouldn't have been possible without the generosity and advice of Carl—and he told him so when Carl commended him on the progress he had made.

"I couldn't have done it without you. I think I'd still be slinging a hammer and framing sun porches if I hadn't met you. And I do want to let you know that I haven't forgotten about the cabin—it just got away from me. Now that I have some breathing space, I can focus on completing that. In fact, I wanted to let you know my plans. At first, I wasn't sure how to use all of the material from your cabin, but now I think I'm ready to proceed and complete my renovations. I plan to take your existing frame and use it to build a second-story loft on my cabin. What do you think?"

"I think it's a fabulous idea, Eric. That's precisely what I wanted—for a piece of the cabin to live on. That's also what I wanted with the experience and knowledge from our mastermind group. You see, knowledge and experience are only valuable if they are used and shared."

"Yes, the tokens. I will keep them close to me at all times and will value their lessons in everything I do."

"Speaking of tokens, Eric, there is one last token that I've been saving until you were ready. But I am not going to send it to you—it is already there. You'll find it when you are done with my cabin, along with a few other items of importance."

"So I have to look for it? A small wooden token among the rubble and remains? What if I overlook it?" Eric asked.

"Don't worry, you won't. For when the student is ready, the teacher will appear. Eric, you have always been ready—you just didn't know it. You'll find the token. I'm sure of that."

After bidding his old friend goodbye, Eric turned to the stack of blueprints on his table. The smaller set represented the addition to his cabin, a project he was anxious to complete in honor of Carl and his grandfather. The second and larger set represented the log cabin house that he was building in Liberty Trails. In the process of developing the site and admiring the homes that had been and were being built, Eric realized that the cabin had a special place in his heart, but it was more appropriate for a weekend or summer home.

Over the course of the last year, he and Heather had started dating and found that they had common interests. When he was entertaining the idea of purchasing one of the lots, he often asked for her opinion in designing the house that would rest on it. By the time the plans were finished, he realized that the plans were a marriage of his ideas with Heather's keen eye and talent. They complemented each other in so many ways that they enjoyed spending as much time together as possible.

Reaching into the box of wooden tokens, he took out another box—a jewelry box that cradled the engagement ring he planned to give her when they broke ground on their new home. He kept the ring with the tokens because to him they were equally special. After all, Eric knew that it was the small old wooden tokens that had made a difference in his life. Without them, there would be no Liberty Trails and he wouldn't have met Heather. In his hands, he held everything he had become and ever would be—in one little box filled with so much.

Chapter 13

Mentorship

A lot can happen in a few years. Not only had Eric become a resident of his first residential development, but he'd also acquired two more developments, each nestled in the surrounding community with a unique theme that paid homage to it.

Heather's father gave his blessing, and they were married shortly after their new home was completed. Max had offered his blessing as well. Then when Eric confided that he wanted to focus solely on residential development, although Max was better known as a commercial and industrial developer, Max assured Eric that he would always be available to offer assistance and advice, but reminded Eric that he was ready to take the next step in his career.

Eric didn't forget his roots. He still loved building things with his own hands and taking pride in quality craftsmanship. It was the hallmark of the reputation he'd built in the community and the reason he was fully involved in each step of dismantling Carl's cabin so it could be moved to its new home, atop his grandather's.

While Eric was a professional builder, the outside walls of log cabins provided him with new challenges, as well as a unique education. Each log had to be removed in a strategic order and numbered so that when it was reconstructed, the grooves would fit perfectly. The fact that it was Carl's cabin made the process even more delicate. Eric wanted to salvage every log that he could, for they had housed the ideas and visions of some very great minds. More than once, Eric pondered what he would hear if those walls could talk.

The process of dismantling Carl's cabin went slower than it should have because Eric wanted to make sure he didn't overlook the last token. He and Heather had gone through the place over and over, searching high and low for the round wooden coin, but it was nowhere to be found. Although Carl had assured him it was there and would present itself, that didn't alleviate his frustration when their searches left them empty handed.

Finally, the last log was removed, and they were down to the foundation. The only other thing remaining was the back porch, which Eric had determined was an addition to the original structure, probably built to accommodate the mastermind groups as they smoked cigars and drank snifters of brandy in the evenings. Thinking of the historical significance of such meetings, Eric was originally reluctant to tear it down, but Carl was adamant that he wanted the property cleared before it was turned over to a real estate broker and put on the market.

Board by board, Eric dismantled the porch by himself. The stack of boards grew quickly, and before long, Eric was down to the wooden floor planks and the steps leading to the flagstone walk that, in turn, led to Carl's favored fishing spot. Slinging his sledge hammer at the top step, he spied a metal box underneath and knew he had his eye on the prize. Scrambling down, he crawled to the side and found an opening large enough to pull it out.

For a few minutes, he simply held it, relishing the anticipation. Then he carefully lifted the lid, listening to its hinges creak after years of being closed and tucked away. Peering inside, he discovered that he had his hands on a treasure, and he quietly carried it to the riverbank, where he sat in Carl's old chair to inspect its contents.

* * *

One year later, Eric cut the ribbon on his own commercial building, the last one he would build. The top floor housed his development company, and Heather's interior design showroom and office were on the floor below. His construction business also had its own dedicated office now, complete with a full staff, including an administrative assistant and bookkeeper. The remaining offices hadn't been difficult to fill.

Eric had been able to rent space to an engineer and surveyor, an architectural firm, and a real estate broker.

His career had been a labor of love, but it hadn't come without struggles and challenges. It had required sweat equity and sacrifice, as well as a willingness to learn that had, at times, made his head spin. It had taken hard work, and it didn't happen overnight. But every lesson and experience had brought him closer to success.

He looked out at the group who had come for today's ribbon-cutting ceremony. In the front row stood Max, who had told Eric he wouldn't miss it for the world. True to his word, he had provided much needed guidance in the design and construction of the five-story building, and his experience had saved Eric from making mistakes more than a few times. Next to Max stood Eric's parents, both beaming with pride at their son's achievements. With a nod, Eric acknowledged the local government officials he'd worked with over the years, and he was touched to see the two veterans who had become his friends after they'd brought the historic battleground to his attention.

The only person missing was his dear friend and mentor, Carl. They had kept in touch via phone calls and emails until Eric received a letter from his wife saying that Carl had passed away peacefully in his sleep. She thanked Eric for giving Carl an opportunity to continue doing what he had so very much loved—using his knowledge and experience to help others succeed and grow. To Carl and his family, his legacy was not of his many accomplishments, but in the wisdom and encouragement he passed on, for that would live forever.

I remember, and I promise I won't forget, Eric thought before reaching for Heather's hand. Together, they picked up the oversized scissors and cut the ribbon, officially opening the doors of the Schultz Building, the new home to their future careers.

After a celebratory lunch and more than a few photographs, the crowd dwindled down. Max patted him on the back and told him how proud he was of him, laughing that he knew him back when....

His parents were busy playing with their granddaughter, Eric's pride and joy. Meredith had been born just 13 months before, and while she was a handful, she was also the apple of her grandparents' hearts. Watching them, Eric realized just how he blessed he was and reached for Heather's hand.

"We should celebrate," he said. "Do you want to go out and have a quiet dinner alone tonight?"

"I have a better idea. How about we make it a weekend? I know a quiet little cabin along the river that would be a perfect getaway. And I don't think we'll have to look very far to find someone who will watch the baby for a couple days," she said, nodding at his parents who were doting on their daughter's every move.

"It's a date," Eric said. "I couldn't think of anything I'd like better.

* * *

Driving up to the cabin, Eric felt a familiar pang as he passed Carl's land. It looked naked without the cabin or any trace of his old friend. That pang turned to gladness as he pulled their SUV into the lane that led to his grandfather's old place. But it didn't look old anymore. The second story loft had been designed to complement the existing structure, and the two blended together as if they were meant for each other. A few steps led to a small porch and the front door, but it was the back of the house that attracted Eric—the addition of a screened-in porch, with a wooden staircase that led to a flagstone walk that took them to the riverbank. It was the perfect place to relax and clear one's mind, and they had spent many weekends there.

Heather laid a blanket on the ground under a weeping willow tree, and they sat quietly, listening to the sounds of nature.

"You know, progress has its benefits," Eric remarked, "but nothing compares to enjoying the basics. It reminds me of simpler times, like when I was a boy and watched my grandfather sit out here."

"He'd be happy to know that you're carrying on the tradition. Eric, he would be so proud of you and what you've done with his cabin. It truly is remarkable—you've even made a country girl out of me!" she laughed.

"I hope Carl would be proud, as well. You know, he was quite remarkable, too, taking a young guy like me under his wing and giving so much of his time and knowledge, without asking for anything in return. I was nothing more than a broke builder who had nothing to offer him in return."

"Oh, yes, you did. You gave him the one thing he had been looking for—you were eager to learn. Remember what his wife said, that Carl's legacy wasn't in his accomplishments or properties or even his bank accounts, but in the legacy he left behind? Eric, your success is his legacy. You gave Carl the opportunity to continue doing what he loved the most—helping others succeed."

"No, Heather, I don't think so. I don't think I'm Carl's final legacy," Eric mused.

"Well, if it's not you, then what is it?"

"It's something that will last long after me. And he left it to me—a box of wooden tokens and a box full of handwritten documents, plans, letters, and ideas that were tucked away under his back porch. That's his legacy. And it was his wish that I would hold onto it and someday pass it on to our children and other aspiring entrepreneurs who could benefit from the experience of him and his mastermind group."

"He left you a box of documents and letters? You never told me that," Heather replied.

"I was waiting for the right moment—the moment when I thought I deserved to be the one to be heir to his treasure. Heather, Carl could have left me millions of dollars, but it still wouldn't have come close to the value of what was in that box. There was even a letter penned by my grandfather on the day he contributed his token to the collection."

"Really? What did it say? What was the token? Come on, inquiring minds want to know."

"Well, first you have to know my grandfather. He wasn't a jovial type, though he was always pleasant to be around. The time we spent together was often quiet, sitting out here on the riverbank with our fishing lines bobbing in the water. I loved every minute, but not because it was fun. I guess it was more because my grandfather treated me as an equal. He didn't tell me what to do or try to make small talk with a young boy. Instead, he shared important things with me, sharing tidbits of his innermost thoughts and wisdom as they popped into his head, just like I was an adult. I felt so important when I was with him. I guess that's why the wooden token that my grandpa left behind means so much to me," he said.

"What was it, Eric?"

"*Mentorship*. You see, every wooden token was contributed by a different member of Carl's mastermind group throughout the years. And every member who contributed one wrote a letter about the principle and why it was important to them. Do you know what my grandfather's letter said?"

"No, tell me," Heather softly replied.

"He said that it was his wish to live long enough to have an impact on my success. In the event he did not, he hoped that the mentorship that the group had shared with each other would be passed on by each member to others who followed in their footsteps. He expressed his belief that knowledge held absolutely no value if it was held captive by a single individual, but he also stated that any knowledge once shared would multiply and become more valuable over time."

"Wow. Do you think Carl specifically chose you when it came time to share the tokens and the knowledge of his mastermind group?" Heather asked.

"I don't know. I'd like to think so. As Carl once said, when the student is ready, the teacher will appear."

"What a story you have to tell our kids one day, Eric. It's really quite amazing how it all came to be," she pointed out.

"The story isn't done yet, Heather. For there is one token that I have yet to implement in his my life and career. I owe it to Carl. I owe it to my grandfather. I owe to the legacy I'll leave my children."

* * *

The spring sun had thawed us out of winter hibernation, and the robins had returned from their southern winter home. The bright green of new grass and leaves colored the surroundings as Eric drove to the cabin. Spring was always a time for new beginnings and growth, and it was his favorite time of the year.

As he drove passed Carl's land one more time, he was surprised to find a vehicle in the drive and what looked to be the beginning stages of construction. On a whim, he pulled into the lane and got out of his truck.

"Hi, I'm Eric Schultz. I own the cabin just down the road. Are you going to be my neighbor?"

"It looks like it. I bought this land last fall and I am going to try my hand at building a summer home here. By the way, I'm Sean," he said, extending his hand.

"It's good to meet you, Sean. It will be good to have someone living here again. And hey, if you need a hand building your summer home, I'll be happy to help. Actually, I started out just like you, energetic and eager to build something with my own two hands," he said, handing the young man his business card.

"You did?"

"I sure did, but wasn't easy. I needed a lot of help and advice, and thankfully, the people I needed were there when I needed them."

"But your card says you're a developer. I can't afford to pay for your help. I appreciate the offer, though," Sean replied.

"No pay necessary. Sometimes you can't put a value on knowledge, Sean. It's something that has no value unless it's given away. I tell you what—why don't you come on over to my cabin. We can sit on the back porch and have a glass of iced tea while you tell me about your plans for this land," Eric offered.

"That'd be great! You don't have to do that, but I sure would appreciate it!"

"Think nothing of it, Sean. Consider it a token of my appreciation for everything that's been given to me. Oh, and don't let me forget to tell you about somebody who was very important to me. His name was Carl."

About the Authors

Dr. Greg S. Reid is published, co-authored, and featured in over 50 books—28 best sellers in 45 countries, five motion pictures, and countless magazines. Greg was hand selected by The Napoleon Hill Foundation to help carry on the teaching found in the bible of personal achievement: *Think and Grow Rich*. One of his greatest accomplishments has been the opportunity to work through American Dream U and support our brave men and women in uniform. He has been a speaker at the Pentagon, Fort Bragg, Fort Hood, and Soldier for Life.

Jeff Levitan was born in Chicago and grew up working in construction and the trades. He graduated from Illinois State University with a finance degree. Today he is a top leader at World Financial Group, which has more than 700 offices and 20,000 insurance and financial service representatives. As a philanthropist, Jeff is also the founder of All for One, a charity that benefits orphans in third-world countries. He lives in Alpharetta, Georgia, with his wife, Cam, and their five children.